Retention
Fundraising

THE NEW ART AND SCIENCE
OF KEEPING YOUR DONORS FOR LIFE

America's All-Time Bestselling Fundraising Books for Securing Major Gifts

Fund Raising Realities Every Board Member Must Face

A 1-Hour Crash Course on Raising Major Gifts for Nonprofit Organizations

David Lansdowne

From the first page, you and your board will be hooked on this one-hour-to-read gem.

The warmth, encouragement, the finely tuned examples and easy readability make for an inviting package that draws you in at once.

Without wasting a word, Lansdowne distills the essence of big-gifts fundraising into 43 "realities" and explains each principle and technique in a way board members will understand instantly.

Put this classic in your board's hands, in their orientation packet, in their annual meeting folder, in their workshop handouts. Put it anywhere you need the art of fundraising illuminated in a masterful, uncomplicated, and engaging way.

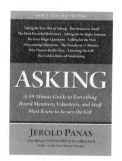

ASKING

A 59-Minute Guide to Everything Board Members, Volunteers, and Staff Must Know to Secure the Gift

Jerold Panas

It ranks right up there with public speaking. Nearly all of us fear it. And yet it's critical to the success of our organizations. Asking for money. It makes even the stout-hearted quiver. But now comes a book, *Asking,* and short of a medical elixir, it's the next best thing for emboldening board members, volunteers, and staff to ask with skill, finesse … and powerful results.

Asking convincingly shows that it doesn't take stellar sales skills to be an effective asker. Nearly everyone can be successful if they follow Panas' step-by-step guidelines.

Emerson & Church, Publishers
www.emersonandchurch.com

Retention Fundraising

THE NEW ART AND SCIENCE
OF KEEPING YOUR DONORS FOR LIFE

Roger Craver

Foreword by Ken Burnett

Emerson
& Church
PUBLISHERS

First printed in September 2014

10 9 8 7 6 5 4 3

Printed in the United States of America
This text is printed on acid-free paper.

Copies of this book are available from the publisher
at discount when purchased in quantity.

Emerson & Church, Publishers
15 Brook Street, Medfield, MA 02052
Tel. 508-359-0019 – Fax 508-359-2703
www.emersonandchurch.com

Library of Congress Cataloging-in-Publication Data

Craver, Roger M.
Retention fundraising : the new art and science of keeping your donors for life / Roger M. Craver.
      pages cm
   Includes bibliographical references.
   ISBN 978-1-889102-53-5 (pbk. : alk. paper)
   1. Fund raising. 2. Philanthropists—Attitudes. 3. Charities—
Management. 4. Nonprofit organizations—Marketing. I. Title.
   HV41.2.C73 2014
   658.15'224—dc23
      2014017259

This book is based on a three-year study
of donor retention and commitment
among 250-plus nonprofits in the U.S. and the U.K.

About the Author

The *Wall Street Journal* described him as "an assassin of all things right-wing." The American Association of Political Consultants placed him in their Hall of Fame, and the Direct Marketing Association gave him their Lifetime Achievement Award.

Roger Craver is, in fact, a disruptor and challenger of the status quo. A pioneer in direct response fundraising in the 60's, telemarketing in the '70s, online information services in the '80s, multi-channel fundraising and communication in the '90s, and donor-designed strategies today, he brings an experienced and critical eye to the greatest problem faced by today's nonprofits: donor retention.

Roger helped launch some of the household names in the nonprofit advocacy sector: Common Cause, Greenpeace, the National Organization for Women, World Wildlife Fund, Habitat for Humanity, and Amnesty International. He helped revitalize and grow older organizations—the ACLU, the NAACP, Sierra Club, Wilderness Society, League of Women Voters, Heifer Project International, and Planned Parenthood.

Roger has conducted capital and annual fundraising campaigns, advocacy and membership drives in the U.S., Canada and throughout Europe.

He continues to challenge conventional thinking through the daily blog *The Agitator* and is currently hard at work disrupting the business-as-usual approach to fundraising through three specialized applied research and analytics firms that provide high quality, automated, inexpensive tools and processes designed to boost donor retention and net income: *DonorTrends*, *DonorVoice*, and *TrueGivers*.

He holds an A.B. from Dickinson College in Carlisle, Pa. and a Doctor of Jurisprudence from the George Washington University National Law Center in Washington, D.C.

Dedication

This book is dedicated to my wife and love Janice Christensen whose generosity, skill and dedication to advancing human rights and dignity is unrelenting. A fervor matched only by her daily question, "Isn't that damn book done yet?"

In fact, Janice doesn't read stuff about fundraising. So if someone doesn't tell her "that damn book's done" she'll continue to believe that I'm still holed up working on my Renaissance romance novel.

Contents

Gratitude

I'm older than most of the trees in the woods outside my window. I make no apologies because one of the advantages of being in this trade for such a long time has been exposure to the wealth of experiences and insights that spring from encountering, working with, and learning from the menagerie of wonderful folks we somewhat loosely label "fundraisers."

Although I accept full responsibility for the content—and the mistakes—in *Retention Fundraising*, it's far more important to expose—and thank—the cast of characters who inspired me to write it . . . those good brains I picked, plagiarized and otherwise took advantage of and those whose insights, critiques, snide remarks and sharp pencils helped get this book over the goal line.

In fact, those involved and to whom I am so grateful are part of an evolutionary chain of practitioners and researchers who care enough about the future of nonprofits to challenge the status quo and put their beliefs into practice day after day. This is an often-thankless task of rolling the fundraising rock of new ideas up the hill. Over and over and over until things change.

Unlike most acknowledgment sections of books, please consider this in many ways the preface because it's important to share with you how I got to this point and who helped or otherwise influenced my thinking.

Meet Kevin.

Frustrated by what I didn't know about retention, I reached out to Greg Schneiders, a first-rate researcher and business partner, with the plea to find and introduce me to a radically different thinker. A thinker with experience beyond the field of fundraising.

Greg introduced me to Kevin Schulman, an expert in consumer attitudes and behavior with an exquisite educational pedigree and work history in applying all of it successfully in the commercial arena.

My instant reaction to his comments were, "That's all well and good, but the nonprofit arena is different"—the typical, dismissive reaction of most of us who work in the sector.

Kevin was indeed radically different from anyone I'd encountered in my career as a consultant, organizer and fundraiser. He had mostly avoided the nonprofit sector while developing customer loyalty strategies for some of the giants of consumer marketing. *Plus, he wore cowboy boots.*

Despite the boots I set aside my first impressions and continued meeting with Kevin. I came to see that not only was he an iconoclast, he was also a brilliant analyst and terrific listener.

At first we didn't agree on much. Our judgments and insights were drawn from entirely opposite perspectives and experiences. His from a deep belief in research findings that I found too reliant on statistics and academic theories. Mine from a mostly intuitive, trust-your-experience approach.

Despite, or maybe because of, our differences, we undertook a three-year period of research looking at donor retention and commitment among 250-plus nonprofits in the U.S. and the U.K.

It's Kevin's work and that of the other DonorVoice team members, Josh Whichard here in the U.S. and Charlie Hulme in the U.K., that provided a new view, through a much-improved lens, that informs the empirical background for this book.

Few people in my career have had a greater impact than Kevin. Nonetheless, I wish he would lose the cowboy boots.

Meet The Agitator

Each weekday morning for the past seven years Tom Belford, co-editor at The Agitator (www.theagitator.net), and I have served up a potpourri of fundraising tips, trends and rants designed to provoke new thoughts and battle complacency among fundraisers.

In recent years it's been quite clear from industry data and from the comments of our readers that the two top problems faced by most nonprofits are "acquisition" and "retention."

So, it didn't take any persuading to enlist Tom's help in designing and promoting a series of research projects in cooperation with DonorVoice to dig deeper into these areas.

Once the research results were in and the book's first draft was extruded from my word processor, it was Tom, with an analyst's heart as objective and cold as that of a Hong Kong jeweler, who tore that first draft apart.

He failed to destroy our 40-year working relationship and in fact bolstered his reputation in my eyes. Thank you Tom.

The Organizer

In 1970 a small band of idealists helped John Gardner start a group called Common Cause. It was the first progressive citizen's lobby built on the belief that a massive movement could be funded by small contributions rather than major gifts from foundations and the wealthy few.

We did it by direct mail and it became the model for dozens of groups that followed: Public Citizen, Environmental Defense, Greenpeace, Amnesty International, the National Organization for Women, and many, many others.

I was in charge of fundraising and Ken Smith was charged with organizing and raising reform issues throughout the U.S., especially California. He did so magnificently.

A few years later we formed Craver, Mathews, Smith & Company to help launch and build groups like NOW, NARAL, Greenpeace and take older groups like The Sierra Club, ACLU, and The League of Women Voters public.

Ken was and is a great partner and fundraiser. Always incisive and direct with his questions. So, I have Ken to thank for wading through and helping to clarify parts of this book. Thank you, Ken.

Meet the Retention Co-Conspirators.

There's a small but mighty band of researchers, practitioners and missionaries whose life's work has made a significant contribution to advancing the understanding of donor relationships and the communications and techniques necessary to strengthen them.

If I fail to include all of those individuals here, hopefully you'll find them in the "Resources" section of the Appendix. (This is exactly why publishing "honor roll" lists in annual reports is so dangerous.)

In 1992, at the height of the inglorious "burn and churn" era of fundraising emerged as The-Heretic-In-Chief, Ken Burnett. His classic, *Relationship Fundraising* (Second Edition, 2002, John Wiley & Sons), suggested that fundraisers should first and foremost be guided by the needs, desires and interests of the donor.

It was Ken's book that started me thinking there must be a way to quantify or codify what he was recommending. Thus began a quest that has taken me 22 years and thankfully Ken has been with me—cajoling, advising and empathizing every step of the way.

Next came Adrian Sargeant with his book (another classic) *Building Donor Loyalty*, co-authored by Elaine Jay (2004, John Wiley & Sons). This well-researched treatise got the ball rolling by demonstrating that there's an empirical, measurable basis for the concept of donor loyalty and commitment.

Although Adrian's hands are clean when it comes to any involvement in *Retention Fundraising*, he's guilty by association 'cause he provided a jumping off or reference point for our research. He continues to provide valuable new research and insights to this day. So, thank you Adrian.

Each quarter for the past decade The Index of National Fundraising Performance, invented by Chuck Longfield, now the Chief Scientist at Blackbaud, has reported on declining acquisition and retention rates. Chuck's benchmark has served as the canary in the coal mine alerting us all to the increasing seriousness of the retention problem.

Chuck does more than document the problem. He's a circuit-riding missionary on the issue and deserves his rightful spot in the Retention Pantheon. Thank you Chuck.

There's no question that a good deal of the problem with retention lies in faulty governance by boards, poor communication with donors and a pervasive incivility in not thanking donors. That's why you'll see a number of references in this book to the work of Simone Joyaux (*Fire Your Lousy Board Members*, 2014, Charity Channel Press), Tom Ahern, (*Making Money from Donor Newsletters*, 2013, Emerson & Church), Lisa Sargeant (The Thank You Letter Clinic found on the Showcase of Fundraising Innovation and Inspiration, www.SOFII.org), and planned giving expert Phyllis Freedman of Smart Giving. We all owe them a shower of gratitude, but I thank them especially for providing examples for this book. Thank y'all.

Like *The Agitator*, there's a daily homily on fundraising copy delivered through the blog, *FutureFundraisingNow.com*, written by Jeff Brooks. Jeff is also the delightfully crusty and realistic author of (*The Fundraiser's Guide to Irresistible Communications*, 2013, Emerson & Church). I've not only relied on and quoted from his insights but he also took the time to read this book's manuscript helping to make it far sharper. Thank you Jeff.

Fraser Green, a Canadian fundraiser and author of *3-D Philanthropy* (2012, Social Sector Press) and I have been riding shotgun to each other for nearly 15 years on the issue of donor loyalty and retention. He's one of the relatively few fundraisers who's both a practitioner and author. In other words he writes the talk, then walks it.

Fraser picked up a quote from a piece on retention I wrote years ago—"Donor Loyalty is the Holy Grail of Fundraising"—and figured he found a fellow traveler. He did and we've been traveling down that road together for a long time. Thank you Fraser.

Of course no fundraising book is worth the paper or the digits it's printed on unless it can be put to practical use. So I turned over the reading and commenting on the manuscript to Craig Lamb of Lamb Consulting whom I've worked with for nearly 25 years.

Craig is one of those quiet unsung heroes who knows what he's doing, has the patience of a saint when dealing with nonprofits, and gets great results. We were in the trenches together years ago with Planned Parenthood, The National Organization for Women and the Democratic Party.

My question to Craig: "Does any of this make practical sense in terms of being put to good use?" He generously raised questions, objections and points of clarification and helped make a better book that will work in real life. Thank you Craig.

It's not easy to put some of these concepts into a graphic rendition. But we live in an age of pictures. To Bill Hendrickson, of BillRossCreative.com who took on this chore, probably thinking it was just another book gig, thank you.

Finally, my editor Jerry Cianciolo has to bear some (a lot) of the responsibility for all this. He's published lots of great fundraising stuff at Emerson & Church. Best of all, he's opinionated as hell. So, I don't have to draw you a map to describe the typography of this relationship.

Fortunately, even as a copywriter I deferred to his kind of expertise and he to mine. Sort of the way things should work in Nonprofit Land, but often don't because so often everyone's an expert in everything.

We're still on speaking terms. Best of all he's produced a readable book for you as opposed to one you simply put on the shelf with all those others you haven't put to use. Thank you Jerry.

Meet the Other Brains I Picked

This book is really not their fault, so don't blame them for how I characterize their work and capture their insights.

There's a group of missionaries out there like Pam Grow, Gail Perry, Kivi Leroux Miller, Nancy Schwartz, Marc Pittman, and Jay Love who hold a special passion in their hearts for helping smaller organizations. Bless them.

The work they do has provided me insights that run throughout this book. Pam, Nancy, Marc, Lisa, Gail and Kivi for their advice on communications delivered in a cost-effective and fundraising-effective manner. Jay, the inventor of e-Tapestry, for now launching a new CRM named Bloomerang that brilliantly focuses on retention using Adrian Sargeant's and Tom Ahern's insights in its design. My thanks to the unsung work they do. Day after day after day.

Then there are practitioners and authors like Canadian Harvey McKinnon who are so sharp that even though their work is tangential to this book it's central to retention. Harvey, for all you do and for your classic on monthly giving *Hidden Gold* (2003, Taylor Trade Publishing), thank you. The same with Sean Trainer, lots of time zones from Harvey, down under at Pareto Fundraising whose missionary work on lifetime value should become a central part of your own fundraising theology. Thanks, Sean.

Finally, there are those individuals in organizations and agencies whose work I follow and who inspire me. Sometimes Tom and

I mention them in the pages of *The Agitator*, sometimes they go unheralded.

People like Mark Phillips, head of Blue Frog in the UK . . . the telemarketing folks at Pell and Bales also in the UK . . . the researchers and data analysts at DonorTrends and True Givers . . . Steve Kerhli at the PETA Foundation . . . Angel Aloma at Food for the Poor. All are integral and major threads of the tapestry that represents my insights into donor retention.

As you've no doubt noticed I don't mention many agencies. That's because they unfortunately don't get paid for retention. But that's another story and I hope compensating agencies for value instead of volume and time will eventually change.

The exception is Craver, Mathews, Smith which I left 10 years ago and in which I have no financial interest. To their credit even without me they persist in underwriting research into donor loyalty.

Meet the Mentors

Of course almost all of our filters are influenced by those we admire. Those who trained and mentored us.

My days are blessed with special and remarkable characters—individuals who are far above the norm in both quality of performance, quality of insight and quality of delivery to their constituents.

Posthumous thanks to John Gardner, who taught me the value of citizen participation and the fact that change will come from the 1% willing to get off their butt at the end of a day's work to attend a meeting, solicit a neighbor or write a member of Congress. To Caesar Chavez, who taught me that "hope" and "persistence" will always win. To Dick Kuch who admonished that "Miracles happen but it's even better to organize for them."

Thanks in the here-and-now to John Glier, of Grenzebach Glier and Associates, whom I view as the premiere philanthropic consultant in the U.S. He understands the true value of donors and has little tolerance for fools or pretenders. To Morris Dees, founder of the Southern Poverty Law Center, who understands human nature and donors better than anyone I've ever known. To Ira Glasser, retired Executive Director of the ACLU who understood the value of a committed donor better than any CEO I've ever met.

Finally, and most importantly, to all the fundraisers in small, mid-sized and large organizations, whom despite the lunacy of some boards and the arrogant incompetence of some CEOs, make things happen.

My singular hope is that I can bring together all you do into a meaningful, actionable whole.

Thank you, one and all.

Roger

P.S. I'm sure I've missed lots of deserving folks. Shame on me. The danger of lists. Please let me know of my egregious error and I'll make sure you're included in the next edition or the next book.

A Website for This Book

The field of empirically-based donor retention is emerging and evolving. Consequently, to keep you updated, and also to provide a place where together we can share ideas and case histories, I've created a related website.

The website is located at www.RetentionFundraising.com. There you'll find detailed information and explanations on subjects related to retention and donor value. "Geek stuff" like formulae, survey questionnaires, and explanations of various models. Far more than I could put in a book—or at least more than my very sane editor would likely accept.

I expect a fair number of challenges and questions so I've enlisted the help of the pros at DonorVoice to keep the site current and the questions answered.

In the spirit of transparency I have both a professional and financial interest in DonorVoice, but assure you the data and recommendations are entirely and objectively divorced from those.

Foreword by Ken Burnett

Our nonprofit sector is bleeding to death. We're hemorrhaging donors, losing support as fast as we find it, seemingly condemned forever to pay a fortune just to stand still.

It's time we stemmed the flow.

Let me say this as simply as I possibly can.

Our sector desperately needs to take decisive, effective action to stem donor attrition. It's costing our causes and all who depend upon them billions of dollars every month. It's limiting, even stifling the great work we do. It's a sure sign of disillusioned, depressed, and deterred donors, our leaking lifeblood. It saps and diminishes our sector, which is a tragedy because we should be society's jewel in this jaded world.

Yet fundraisers routinely put up with it, as if attrition were a fundraising fact of life.

It isn't. Roger Craver says so. I'm sure he's right.

Here, in your hands, you now hold the answer to this gargantuan, ongoing catastrophe. The big question—now that you know the problem and you've grasped the potential solution—is can you—yes, you reading this page now—do anything about it?

What a horrible word it is, *attrition*. It means wasting away. How can it be that, faced with the urgency, glamour, drama, and shining righteousness of the needs we exist to address and the opportunities that we give donors to make a difference, how can our supporters abandon us by the shed-load, often after the briefest of acquaintance, seemingly content to leave us at the drop of a hat?

How did we ever allow this?

I've been acquiring and working to retain donors for thirty-seven years. One thing's been constant throughout that time: fundraising's gotten steadily more expensive. In this simple equation lies the seed of our destruction.

Under-investment. The classic fundraising false economy. We've no choice but to spend ever more to bring in new donors, so we under-invest in keeping existing donors inspired, comfortable, and happy.

What on earth have we been thinking?

Roger Craver's book could scarcely be more timely. Let's use it as a rallying call. Our sector doesn't need more pundits, number crunchers, data geeks, social media gurus, or consultants. These people are ten a penny, and their impact has been limited at best. What we need are world-changers.

Cracking donor retention is a worthy challenge for any would-be world-changer. As this book shows, there's so much for him or her to tackle.

- Switch the focus from past transactions to ongoing commitment.
- Find what matters most to donors.
- Remove all the retention barriers—see chapter 16.
- Identify committed donors. Delight them regularly.

- Do everything much more quickly.
- Give great feedback.
- Invest in retention.

The list goes on. They're all detailed in this book.

As Roger shows, the formula for fundraising magic is simple: retention + commitment = increased lifetime value. It isn't a wild dream. We just have to be as committed to it as we'd wish our donors would be to us.

The leaking bucket is a sign of monumental failure in our profession. All who preside over such pallid performance deserve to be fired. Really. Unless you're ready to change this picture, move over, get out of the way, and give your place to someone who can implement the change our sector so desperately needs.

In chapter 18 of *Retention Fundraising*, Roger features the random mystery shopping tests that for years people like me have carried out on charities. Posing as potential donors we've tested shortcomings such as response times, thanking, delivery on promises, knowledge, passion, and whether a charity's communications are donor and beneficiary focused rather than obsessed with the organization.

These tests always produce the same dismal, dire results. Fundraisers, generally, are inept at customer service and seem incapable of learning how to change. This isn't just shortsighted, it's a disgrace. Mostly, it's because fundraisers simply don't prioritize donor retention or invest in it adequately. If your CEO and board don't grasp the financial benefits of giving donors a brilliant experience, change your board and CEO, or change your job.

Our enterprises don't need Cassandras and merchants of doom. Instead we need optimistic prophets. We may be the nonprofit sector, but we can't afford to be without our prophets. As Roger Craver shows, the solution is not rocket science. We could change this circumstance now, really we could. It's our duty to all the causes we serve: we must not persist in hemorrhaging donors.

So what's missing? What is the lost link between the vitally urgent tasks we exist to address and retention, our ability to keep donors with us long enough to get the job done?

Roger Craver has found the answer. It's in these pages. For this, we should be hugely grateful.

If you agree that the time has come to change fundraising's retention paradigm, you can make a start now by reading this book.

But please, when finished, don't file its ideas away on your bookshelf. Put them into action throughout your nonprofit, now.

Ken Burnett,
London EC

PART 1

What Is Retention, and Why Is It Important?

Time for Change

I'll never forget the little old lady.

Early in my career I called on her to discuss the college's plan for a new library, hoping she'd become a major contributor.

She served tea and little cucumber sandwiches. We chatted amiably and then got down to business. With great enthusiasm I showed her the architect's schematics, explained why it was a sound idea to raze the old dorm that had stood for ninety years, and how attractive the new library would be in its place.

My confidence grew as she took it all in. She asked bright, incisive questions and didn't wince when I suggested the amount of a gift that would represent her share of the project.

"Young man," she said as I concluded, "I'm very impressed. But I won't be contributing to this project."

I was startled. "May I ask why not?"

"Well, you see, I'm all in favor of progress, but I'm absolutely opposed to change."

All too many of our organizations are like that little old lady. We claim we're in favor of income growth and a sustainable future. But in practice we ignore the huge fundraising changes that threaten both.

We blithely continue doing the same old things, ignoring the eventual and inevitable day of reckoning.

Surprise! That day has already arrived.

Year after year for the past decade, donor-retention rates have been sinking. Today they're at an all-time low.

In a 2013 study by the Association of Fundraising Professionals, only 65 of the 2,377 organizations surveyed had a retention rate over 70 percent! (Sadly, the study contained no profiles of the 65 high-retention organizations.)

That same study also found:

Flat Fundraising. Every $100 raised from new donors was offset by $100 in losses.

Negative growth in the number of donors. For every 100 donors acquired, 107 were lost through attrition.

Small organizations suffering most. On average, charities raising more than $500,000 lost $90 for every $100 raised. Those raising between $100,000 and $500,000 lost as much as they gained. And organizations raising $100,000 or less lost $110 for every $100 raised.

In brief, the days of the seemingly infinite pool of new donors available to quickly and inexpensively replace those who've stopped their support are long gone.

Today, as more and more donors abandon ship, the cost of replacing them has grown so great as to be no longer affordable for most nonprofits.

It doesn't have to be this way. Consider this:

The average nonprofit has a 60–70 percent chance of obtaining additional contributions from existing donors; a 20–40 percent probability of securing a gift from a recently lapsed donor; *but less than a 2 percent chance of receiving a gift from a prospect.*

With these figures in tow, you'd think we'd be pouring the bulk of our marketing and fundraising dollars into *retaining* donors, rather than laying out large sums to acquire more and more new ones.

But sadly we're not. Too many of our boards, CEOs, and fundraisers haven't accepted the new reality of a world that's never going to return to the good old days.

Fortunately, there is good news. There's a proven process now for increasing donor retention—for plugging the holes in the bucket through which our donors are pouring.

This process outlined in this book is based on empirical evidence we gathered in partnership with Kevin Schulman and his team at DonorVoice. You can learn more about the research in chapters of Part 3.

By understanding and putting this process to work, we can add tens of thousands or even millions of dollars to our organizations' bottom lines.

All that's required is adopting new mindsets, new metrics, and new methods—all of which we can learn quickly and start to apply immediately.

There are two metrics that are especially important—*retention rate* and *lifetime value* (LTV). These are fundamental measures of how well your organization is performing in the eyes of donors. You'll find a detailed explanation of these metrics in chapters 20 and 21, but in short, the definition of *retention rate* as used in this book is the percentage of all donors who give in two consecutive years, and *lifetime value* is the total multi-year donors have contributed over time.

Why the CFO Will Love You

If you question whether it's worth devoting a substantial part of your professional time to mastering donor retention, here's a great illustration from Chuck Longfield, the founder of Target Analytics and Blackbaud's chief scientist.

Chuck's a committed and talented pro who's spent nearly thirty years benchmarking and monitoring nonprofit vital signs.

Once upon a time . . . there was a CFO who came before the board and reported:

> "Last year you authorized me to invest $100,000 in building our endowment. I'm happy to report I lost $75,000—75 percent of the money I invested."

Eyebrows raised.

"Now," continued the CFO, "I'm back again this year to ask for another $100,000 so I can follow the same strategy."

You can imagine how long that CFO would last in the real world.

Sadly, this isn't a fairy-tale scenario. It happens in thousands of organizations year after year.

Collectively we pour hundreds of millions of dollars into acquiring new donors, only to find our investment evaporating as donors exit by the thousands during the first year.

No wonder so many CFOs have problems with high investments in acquisition campaigns. They see money pouring out of the leaky bucket in ever increasing torrents.

If you want to know why your CFO (and CEO and Board and your colleagues) will love you by solving the problem of retention just take a look at the chart below. See what a significant difference retention rate makes.

The illustration below shows the 5 year income difference between average retention rates of 41%, 51%, and 61% a year over a 5 year period for an organization with 10,000 donors giving an average gift of $45 each year.

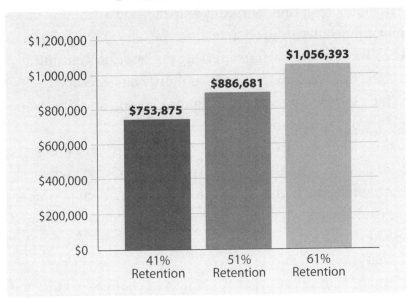

CUMULATIVE INCOME OVER FIVE YEARS

Why Has It Taken So Long to Focus on Retention?

When it comes to the best methods for acquiring donors, there's a fifty-plus-year history of tested and proven general principles to guide us. Not so in the case of improving retention and increasing donor value.

Although the commercial world has spent billions of dollars and three decades successfully figuring out its customers, we in the nonprofit sector have largely relied on the thinking, insights, and powerful intuition of such practitioners as Ken Burnett, whose seminal work *Relationship Fundraising*, first published in 1992, opened eyes with its insights and advice.

Fifteen years later, in 2004, came Adrian Sargeant's and Elaine Jay's *Building Donor Loyalty: The Fundraiser's Guide to Increasing Lifetime Value,* a well-researched treatise outlining the factors that drive donor retention. Sargeant and Jay explained how to keep donors committed to an organization and offered suggestions, supported by case studies, for increasing donor value over time.

Alas, this wise advice has fallen mostly on deaf ears.

The practices of most organizations remain stuck in the good old days of "burn and churn" donor acquisition.

Days when donors could actually be acquired at a profit.

Days when little attention was paid to the loss of donors.

After all, why bother so much with current donors when new ones could be gathered quickly and cheaply enough to replace the "ingrates" who left?

That was then.

Today the nonprofit landscape has changed significantly, but unfortunately the organization-centric mindset prevails. It's ingrained in current practices.

Let's see if we can play a quick game of catch-up.

Losing Donors Through
the Leaky Bucket

There's no better starting point in planning and building your organization's future than by taking essential steps to hold onto as many of your donors as possible.

A simple diagram makes it easy to describe and understand the issues we're dealing with:

LOSING DONORS THROUGH THE LEAKY BUCKET

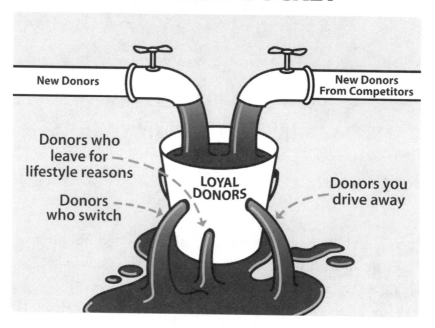

The bucket is your fundraising program. Donors flow into it through two faucets. New donors enter through the left. They heard about you from a friend, received a piece of direct mail, saw something about you on the news, or checked out your website. Good work. You have a new donor.

Other donors flow into your bucket from the right faucet. They aren't crazy about your competition and decided to leave when they saw your direct mail piece or heard about you. In short, your competition didn't please them. Maybe you will.

One of three things will happen while these new donors are in your bucket:

1. They'll stay and become loyal supporters. Count them as part of your committed base of donors. Nice going.
2. They'll leave . . . by dying, moving, changing their interest, or because of a lifestyle change such as illness or retirement.
3. They'll switch to another organization either because they've changed their focus from the issue you're involved with to a new set of issues, or because they didn't find the love they wanted from you. If they're not leaving because of a change in issue interests, then most often it's because of something you did or didn't do. Shame on you.

When you put the faucets and the bucket together, here's how the processes of donor acquisition and donor retention work in tandem:

- Your marketing—direct mail, advertising, communications, and online strategy—regulates the quality and intensity of the flow of new donors into the bucket.
- The size of the hole through which donors exit is determined by the quality of experiences you provide while they're in your bucket.

The long-term success of your organization is determined by the relationship between the flow in and the flow out, and by keeping as many donors as possible in the bucket for as long as possible.

Sadly, most groups concentrate far more on pouring new donors into the bucket than on plugging the holes.

Why Donors Leave

I'd just made what I felt was a mighty effective case for a major gift from the CEO of a Fortune 500 company and was absolutely startled when he said, "No, I won't give!"

I was nonplussed. "May I ask why?"

His response: "Because of minced pie."

A bit dumbfounded, I eventually found my tongue. "What does minced pie have to do with giving to our alma mater?"

"Nothing," he said. "But when you don't want to give, one excuse is as good as another."

Fortunately, when it comes to donor defection, there aren't many "minced-pie" reasons for leaving. In general, we know why donors stop giving, and it's possible for every organization to identify the specific reasons donors quit it.

Take a moment to study the infographic below. It details the reasons why donors leave compared to the reason consumers walk away from businesses.

It's worth exploring in some detail the reasons donors leave:

5%—Thought the charity didn't need them. Clearly, if you don't tell donors about your needs, or, better yet, the beneficiaries you help, why should they bother staying with you? After all, they joined because they wanted to help.

8%—No information on how monies were used. There are two key questions donors ask: 1) Why do you need my help? and 2) Did my contribution make any difference? Fail to answer these two questions, and you'll lose your donors. This will increasingly be the case as more skeptical "show-me" Baby Boomers and Generations Y and X come to the fore. Remember: if you neglect to tell 'em, there are thousands of other organizations that will.

9%—No memory of supporting. If ever there were evidence of ineffective communication and branding, this is it. If you don't help a donor distinguish your organization from

Handwritten margin notes:
★
· Appeal TY Notes
- Follow up cards
- Story Cards

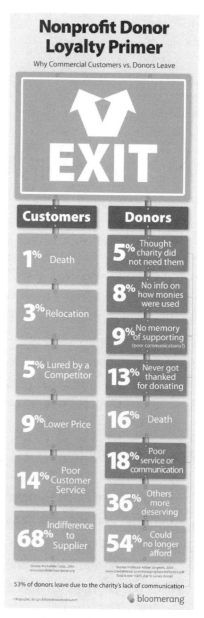

Nonprofit Donor Loyalty Primer

Why Commercial Customers vs. Donors Leave

Customers		Donors	
1%	Death	5%	Thought charity did not need them
3%	Relocation	8%	No info on how monies were used
5%	Lured by a Competitor	9%	No memory of supporting (poor communications?)
9%	Lower Price	13%	Never got thanked for donating
14%	Poor Customer Service	16%	Death
68%	Indifference to Supplier	18%	Poor service or communication
		36%	Others more deserving
		54%	Could no longer afford

Source: Rockefeller Corp., 2006
www.rockefellerfoundation.org

Source: Professor Adrian Sargeant, 2000
www.combatbreaker.com/managingdonordefection.pdf
Total is over 100% due to survey design

53% of donors leave due to the charity's lack of communication

infographic design: bloomnetcreative.com   🔴 bloomerang

Source: Bloomerang.co
(Total is greater than 100 percent due to survey design.)

others, you're likely to be forgotten. Generalized or aspirational taglines such as "We work hard to feed the hungry" or "We offer excellence in a multi-cultural environment" serve only to reinforce donor amnesia.

13%—*Never got thanked for donating.* Failure to thank a donor properly is bad manners *and* horrible fundraising. No act of omission more clearly signals, "We don't care. Just send the money." Is it any surprise that organizations that behave rudely don't hold onto their donors?

The failure to thank donors properly is so grievous I've devoted an entire section to it (see chapter 17).

16%—*Death.* No surprise here. Donors tend to be far older than the general population. Notice that the commercial world, with far, far younger consumers, loses only 1percent because of mortality. If, however, you've treated your donors well, a small but special group will make their largest contributions at the end of life in the form of bequests or other planned gifts.

18%—*Poor service or communication.* Relative to the minutiae we obsess about—the logo, the annual report, the mission statement—too many of us just don't grasp why spelling a donor's name correctly or promptly responding to inquiries and complaints is so important. We mistakenly treat donor service as a cost center, when in reality good service can add thousands, tens of thousands, or hundreds of thousands to the bottom line.

36%—*Others more deserving.* This statistic screams *failure* on the part of fundraising and communications departments. With more than a million groups clamoring for support, organizations

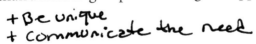

+ Be unique
+ Communicate the need

that don't state a powerful case leave themselves wide open to donors defecting to similar groups.

54%—*Could no longer afford.* This may be the mince-pie excuse in this lineup of reasons why donors stop their support. Experience shows that organizations that make strong cases and provide positive experiences usually avoid being cut as donors trim the list of groups they support due to changes in health, retirement, or reduction in income.

Do you note a pattern or common thread in these reasons for defection? With the exception of death and a donor's personal financial situation, every one is entirely within the control of your organization. That's right, organizations through their own actions—or inactions—are jeopardizing their own retention rates.

There's an exception that applies particularly to advocacy organizations. Sometimes donors simply decide to change their priorities moving from, say, handgun control to human rights. When this happens there's not much you can do.

Let's turn now to exploring *why* an organization itself ultimately determines its own retention rate.

PART 2

Setting the Stage for Improved Retention

5

Confessions of a Fundraiser: Why I Changed

For nearly a decade Tom Belford, my co-editor at The Agitator (www.theagitator.net), and I have voiced our concern over falling acquisition rates and declining retention rates. We've been especially obsessed with the latter.

And for years as a consultant I strove in every way I could to implement Ken Burnett's recommendations on donor-relationship management and Adrian Sargeant's findings on donor loyalty.

In retrospect, I believe I offered good advice and insights to my clients. When it came to such activities as acquisition and upgrading, I relied on empirically proven formulae. But as far as retention was concerned, I followed my hunches. There wasn't an empirical framework to follow.

Certainly, I knew from Adrian's research that improving donor commitment—he labels it *loyalty*—was financially valuable. And I was well aware from Ken's treatise on the host of donor-centric actions organizations could take to improve their donors' loyalty and commitment.

What I didn't know exactly—and all these unanswered questions were driving me crazy—was what specific actions would actually lead to greater loyalty/retention/commitment, and which actions weren't worth the effort.

Sure, I understood the importance of proper and effective acknowledgments or thank-yous and a solid welcoming process for new donors. Not to mention the need to show what great things the donors' contributions made possible.

But what about publications? A lot of organizations spend thousands on newsletters and magazines. Do these really matter? If so, how much?

How about the ways in which donor inquiries and complaints are handled? Does that count for much? And reporting on the organization's mission progress and results? Just how important is it, and how is it best done?

So, with a headful of questions, I set out with Kevin Schulman and his skilled team at DonorVoice (www.thedonorvoice.com) on a quest to unearth the answers.

The data-based, empirical framework we developed for boosting retention and increasing lifetime value is summarized and applied in the chapters that follow. It is based on studies of thousands of donors to more than 250 nonprofit organizations in the United States, Canada, and the United Kingdom.

Much of what we learned will surprise you.

6

Thinking Differently to Improve Retention

"What are you doing differently today to improve retention?"
I've had the opportunity to ask a number of fundraisers this question. Here's a sampling of the answers I've heard most often:

"We're going to do a test using content marketing—no ask, more visuals, fewer touches or contacts with the donors."

"We're doing a big push on acquisition to build momentum for file growth."

"We've identified who's likely to give, upgrade, and lapse. We know who's best to pursue for conversions to monthly giving and who are the most predisposed to lapsing."

Each of these answers has some traits in common:

All tend to be tactical, meaning they focus on techniques such as frequency of asking, the types of graphics used, the pace or volume of communications.

All represent the act of throwing money at the retention problem in a scattershot manner.

All are focused exclusively on activities undertaken by the fundraising/marketing department. Little or no focus on donor service. Little or no thought on how best to relate programs and mission to the donor.

All place considerable emphasis on the *who* (the audience) but little attention to the *why* (donor attitudes for giving or leaving) or *what* (experiences that will affect donor attitudes).

All are examples of winning the battle only to lose the war, because, unfortunately, none is rooted in what causes donor commitment or loyalty and what really boosts retention.

Here's the type of answer I wish I had heard more often:

"We've identified five changes that we're now making. We project these changes will add $374,000 in revenue at zero additional cost. They include focusing on our two core messages that matter most to donors and not the other four we've also been using.

"We're also eliminating two publications that add no value for our donors; improving our first-call resolution in the donor services department; setting up a donor feedback program on our website and in donor services to address problems when they occur and build relationships in real time.

"By eliminating activities that don't matter to donors and improving those that do, we're creating a meaningfully different experience for our most loyal donors and deriving significantly more revenue from them with no mid-level or major gift officer required."

Fanciful? Hardly.

The fact is the response above reflects the fundamental reality of building donor loyalty and commitment. You can't use business-as-usual tactics to stumble your way to a solution. You can't throw money willy-nilly at the problem through a series of techniques and tactics. And you certainly can't target your way to a solution through conventional segmentation of your donor base.

The only way to arrive at a truly effective, results-producing retention solution like the one outlined here is to identify—and scale—the experiences that positively affect your donors' commitment and repair or eliminate those that don't.

Understanding Relationships

Fixing the problem of donor loss begins with understanding some fundamentals about relationships in general and more specifically how these fundamentals apply to donors.

There is a sizable body of work by academics and practitioners who've devised a framework called *relationship theory* to determine and describe the dynamics and essential ingredients of both personal and commercial relationships.

Hands-on experience and decades of research make clear that the underlying elements constituting a healthy interpersonal relationship—the one you have with your best friend, your spouse or partner, and trusted colleagues at work—also apply to relationships in business to business (B2B), business to consumer (B2C), and nonprofit to donor (N2D).

(I've included in the Appendix a list of resources on relationship theory should you wish to learn more about it.)

The Twin Pillars Supporting a Solid Relationship

There are two key pillars that go into creating a positive nonprofit-to-donor relationship, the very kind that leads to higher loyalty, commitment, and retention:

Functional Connection.

The journey begins with the desire on the donor's part to establish a basic (what social scientists call *functional*) connection with your organization.

The main characteristics of a successful functional connection are reliability and consistency. The donor comes to know what he or she can reliably expect from you, and that experiences with your organization are consistent.

For example, you acquire a first-time donor using a powerful message to save the baby seals. It's reasonable to assume the donor has a special regard for animals, in this case baby seals. So your follow-up appeals would naturally focus on your work in this area. That would be consistent. What you shouldn't do is acknowledge the donor's original gift with an equally powerful message about the dangers of plutonium and then follow up with a well-crafted appeal to help stop strip mining. There's no consistency there. And chances are, no additional gifts.

Or, say John Smith sends in his first check. His acknowledgment reads, "Dear John Smythe." He calls and requests the spelling of his surname be corrected and is met with the uncaring voice of a rude clerk.

No reliability. No additional gifts.

If your organization fails to deliver both reliable and consistent experiences, you will fail at retention. Period.

Conversely, when you achieve a solid level of functional connection, the donor's level of trust allows you to move to the next, vitally important tier of the relationship.

Personal Connection.

This is the more emotional part of the relationship. Personal connections are actions you take to make the donor feel an important part of the cause—things such as giving recognition, seeking the donor's opinion, sending timely and relevant communications, and offering other forms of involvement.

In the vernacular of the social scientists, personal connection is the *fidelity* part of a relationship. The bond saying there's a two-way street of give and take, of mutual respect, with the donor believing the organization knows him or her and truly cares.

Below is a diagram showing how the main types of donor experiences combine to build commitment.

CAUSES OF A STRONG RELATIONSHIP

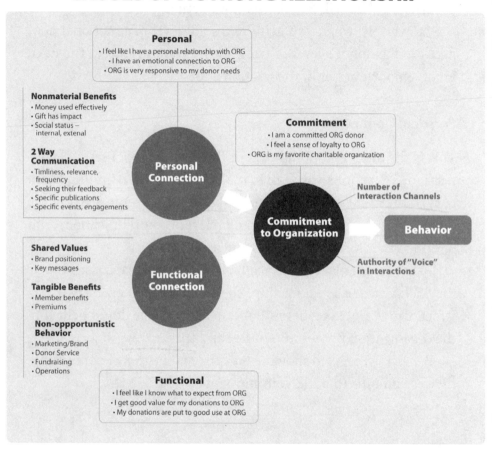

When donors are both functionally satisfied and personally connected to your organization, they recommend you to others, stay with you, and are willing to forgive the occasional mistake (the two-month lapse in correcting the spelling of a name, for example). In short they trust you because your actions have demonstrated you care about their needs.

All this adds up to "trust" and that's the linchpin.

8

Eliminating Guesswork by Redefining Loyalty

Retention occurs only when fundraisers, communications personnel, donor service managers, program officers, CEOs, and board members—everyone in the organization—understands why donors stay or leave and what steps can be taken to keep them.

Historically, most of us have based our actions on the donor's transactional behavior. By that I mean we focus on the recency of a donor's contribution, the frequency of his or her gifts, and the amounts he or she has given.

In the jargon of our trade, this combination of behaviors is referred to as *RFM*. It's one of the most commonly used metrics in fundraising.

We use RFM as a proxy or substitute measure of loyalty. We assume that a donor who gives frequently, in generous amounts, and has made a recent gift is likely to be highly loyal and will, therefore, have a high retention rate and ultimately a high value.

The Problem with RFM

To understand why relying on transactional behavior (RFM) won't get you far in terms of improving donor retention rates, let's begin with the definition of *loyalty*.

> **Loy-al-ty:** 1: The state or quality of being loyal.
> 2: A feeling or attitude of devoted attachment and affection.

=emotional

Pay particular attention to the phrase "a feeling or *attitude of devoted attachment.*" This is *the* essential ingredient in understanding retention.

The problem with focusing only on transactional behavior is that it represents a snapshot of the *past.* It offers no insights as to the cause and effect of your donor's behavior, and cause and effect are exactly what you need to understand.

It is the actions of an organization that *cause* the good (or poor) donor attitude. And, the resulting *effect* of good attitude is donor behavior reflected in more giving, more commitment, higher retention, and greater lifetime value.

That's why using transactional behavior to define loyalty or commitment is like trying to grow a tree by watering its leaves. The focus is on the wrong end of the plant.

Too many of us accept an oversimplified set of generic best practices as sufficient for causing donor behavior—the "thank-you within 48 hours," the assumed importance of the welcome kit, the quality of the creative, and the benefits offered, such as newsletters, magazines, giving clubs, and special events.

I'm not saying these activities are bad per se. Rather, I'm emphasizing that you can't assume that, just because you're offering a range of experiences similar to those offered by other organizations, your retention rates and donor loyalty will automatically improve.

This point of view leads to a commoditized offering that is properly labeled *organization-centric*. It's a counterproductive point of view, if for no other reason than it focuses primary attention and the bulk of marketing resources on techniques, tactics, and volumes rather than on understanding whether or not they positively affect donor attitudes and, if so, why.

If results weaken, we reason, we can solve the problem with more mailings, bigger or smaller envelopes, better creative, or more premiums.

Even if you execute perfectly on these transactional techniques and tactics, they aren't the only or even the best tools for improving donor loyalty and your organization's retention rates.

9

Barriers to Retention

We fundraisers love lists. Most are of the "Top Five Steps to Success" variety. Frankly, I've always been more intrigued with the "Top Five Steps NOT to Take."

Just as someone who's just learning to ride a bike wouldn't attempt to mount it wearing a 40-pound backpack or peddle with flat tires, there are several things you shouldn't do when it comes to retention. I call them *retention barriers.*

If you're serious about increasing retention and donor value, you'll do everything in your power to eliminate or at least lower these barriers.

Retention Barrier 1: Silos

These days the term *multichannel integration* seems to account for more ink, conference bookings, and webinar time than any other concept in our field. It's clear evidence of the assumed importance of the web, social media, streaming video, and other new media, and the mobile phones, tablets, and other hardware that deliver them.

But if so many are touting the glory of this new fundraising heaven, why are so few actually making it through the pearly gates of multichannel integration to receive its everlasting rewards?

In a word: silos. Or more specifically, the information silo, which is by far the biggest organizational barrier to effective donor retention.

Those who work in organizations with more than one department are familiar with the daily manifestation of silos. The online personnel do little to coordinate with the offline folks. Major gift officers look down on direct mail fundraisers and vice versa. Communications people and fundraisers are seldom on the same page where messaging is concerned. And everyone ignores the donor service workers.

The result: a fundraising/communications/donor care system that is incapable of reciprocal interaction and reinforcement, one that drives away donors.

Remember that *consistency* is an essential element for building a solid relationship? If ever there were an enemy of consistency, it's the silo.

Example: the direct mail department brings in a new donor with a powerful message of saving baby seals. The online department sends an e-mail thanking the donor for his or her gift but ignoring any mention of seals and emphasizing the organization's work on climate change. A week later the organization's newsletter arrives touting the importance of saving wetlands.

There's little chance the new donor will stick around. At the very moment the organization needs to be building trust, it undermines itself with inconsistency.

Happily, a number of enlightened CEOs are waking up and taking action. Such groups as the Humane Society of the United States, Operation Smile, Child Fund International, American Cancer Society, and St. Jude have created entire departments of trained professionals focused on donor care and experience. Some even have, by whatever title, created the position of chief donor officer.

I can't think of a more important new position in today's multichannel world. By identifying and giving authority to a person who's responsible for integration—one with line authority across various departments—the organization is signaling that its top priority is providing the donor with what he or she wants and needs.

Retention Barrier 2: False attribution

We'll never make much progress solving the retention problem until we rid ourselves of the myopic and wrongheaded metrics used to measure and reward success in holding onto donors and increasing their value.

Part of the problem is a fundamental misunderstanding of the term *attribution*. In terms of retention and lifetime value, it means assigning performance results to various actions or sources. As in, which factors (message, donor service, communications, thank-yous, donor recognition) contribute in what proportion to increasing or decreasing the lifetime value of a donor base.

Unfortunately, for too many organizations attribution amounts to little more than the annual or semi-annual internal battle over who gets credit for the proceeds from various *fundraising* efforts. How much did the renewal program bring in? What about the appeals and reinstatement campaigns? Immediate money, not long-term value, is the misplaced metric used too often.

This is where the problem with retention begins. When it comes to the metric that matters most—improving lifetime value—our research shows that the tactics, techniques, or frequency of campaign activity from the fundraising department accounts for less than 20 percent of the ultimate value of a donor Nowhere in this type of calculation is value assigned to the donor service department or the work of the program and communications staffs.

Despite the obvious value of viewing this process holistically, fundraisers and their consultants continue to insist on overvaluing single campaign activities and attributing results in a campaign-by-campaign, transactional approach. "Hooray, the October appeal was gangbusters, guess our great recency, frequency, monetary value selection was the reason for its success."

Meanwhile, important ongoing activities that add real and lasting value (proper thank-you and welcome programs, donor-centric newsletters, extraordinary donor service) are discounted or ignored.

To put it another way, the current approach to attribution radically skews value by focusing only on a handful of organizational actions (e.g., the e-mail and direct mail appeal from a single campaign) and biases everything toward short-term campaign metrics.

Did the well-constructed thank-you letter to donors of the appeal preceding campaign X have no impact on their subsequent decision to give to campaign Y?

And what about the massive number of non-responders to campaign X? What if the message used actually hurt retention and subsequent giving? Shouldn't the fundraising team, always clamoring for credit, receive a negative attribution for harming retention and lifetime value?

My goal in raising these issues is simple: to encourage you to consider the collective actions of everyone in your organization. It is the sum of these organization-wide activities that will determine whether your donors stay or go.

A brief and graphic illustration of how the attribution process should work can be found in a short retention quiz and screencast at the book's website: www.retentionfundraising.com/retention-quiz/

Retention Barrier 3: Differentiation

Apart from those who literally die and those whose incomes shrink, your defecting donors don't simply retire from charitable giving. They most likely give to something else, and usually in the same sector! They don't typically switch from cancer research to Greenpeace, in other words.

In chapter 4 we saw that 36 percent of all donors who leave—roughly one out of three—hit the exit because they find other organizations more deserving.

To put it another way, when you fail to provide experiences that reflect your donors' aspirations and values, they simply meet these needs by giving to another group.

That's why paying attention to such mundane activities as donor service is critical.

Another essential donor experience—one often overlooked—pertains to the quality of the creative, copy writing, and messaging processes.

When you fail to differentiate your organization as the best vehicle for meeting the donor's aspirations—in other words, when you don't appear much different from the competition—you've entered a zone of sameness where, with the exception of its name, your organization is indistinguishable from others. And donors who can't distinguish one group from another aren't especially committed. They'll easily switch their giving.

Given the plethora of mailing list exchanges, cooperative donor databanks, and look-alike direct mail packages focusing on technique rather than message and mission, is there any wonder so many donors move from one organization to the next?

As long as copycat fundraisers continue to order up yet more certificates of appreciation, plush toys, sets of labels, matching gift challenges—you name it—while at the same time ignoring dull but basic actions such as top donor service and distinctive messaging, what reasons do donors have to stick around?

Precious few, if any. So when the next environmental (pick any sector you want) appeal, looking and sounding virtually the same as the ten others slated for their mailbox this month, arrives, it's not surprising that donors feel free to switch.

Where there is weak or no brand recognition there's likely to be poor retention. Put another way, where there is no brand identification there is churn. And where there's churn there's always lousy retention.

How bad is it? Consider this: Many organizations find that using their logos in acquisition mailings *depresses* response when compared to a blank envelope.

If McDonald's or J.Crew or Starbucks discovered they could get more customers and sell more products by suppressing their identity, they'd consider it a crisis of catastrophic proportions.

Unfortunately, too many of our nonprofits are willing to accept that, where their brands are concerned, there are only generic coffee shops, clothing stores, and burger joints. No Starbucks, Caribou, McDonald's, Wendy's, or Burger Kings.

Lay before you five health-care, five environmental, five disease or human services packages. Black out the names of the organizations and see if you can distinguish one from the other. You'll soon understand how best practices have resulted in an undifferentiated sea of sameness.

Donors see this phony array multiple times a week or month. And we wonder why retention rates are down.

Please take all of the above to heart, but don't interpret what I'm saying as a recommendation to run out and find a whiz-bang brand master to create some new concept—logo, name, tagline—in the hope it'll solve your differentiation problem. If history is any guide, you're more likely than not to end up with some brain-dead, revenue-crushing alternative.

Retention Barrier 4: Premiums and tchotchkes

It may take a while, but most of us in fundraising come to realize that over-reliance on tchotchkes, baubles, and other gifts to boost response rates is a long-term prescription for poor retention and reduced lifetime value.

There's a reason some jokingly refer to premiums as "the crack cocaine of fundraising." The analogy is literally true. Scientists, using controlled experiments, have determined that extrinsic rewards activate the same part of the brain and same chemical (dopamine) as does cocaine.

When donors are offered a premium, their focus changes to the self-interested question of what's in it for them rather than the benefit that springs from altruism. This is why the hoped-for conversion from a premium donor to normal donor seldom happens.

Does this mean you should forgo all gifts? Absolutely not! Some organizations successfully use "lite" premiums such as address labels and note cards (as opposed to watches, umbrellas, stuffed animals) in acquisition mailings but never use them again once the donor is on board.

And a great strategy for building commitment and retention among your existing donors is to occasionally offer a gift directly linked to your mission or program. Photos from the field . . . a book authored by the CEO . . . a DVD of a cultural event.

But don't tie your gift to a request for funds. Surprise donors with it as a thank-you for their support, perhaps on the anniversary of becoming a donor, perhaps in celebration of a particular victory their support has helped make possible. The gift will serve as a reminder of shared purpose and mission and the donors' important role in achieving it.

For doubters who persist in believing quid pro quo is somehow more effective when it comes to giving, note the findings from an experiment in the world of blood donation:

Researchers visited a regional blood center and found 153 women ready to give blood. The 153 were randomly divided into two groups. One group was told the blood donation was voluntary and no payment would be received. The second was told they'd receive 50 Kroners (about $9) for their blood.

Guess what happened? Fifty-three percent of the first group, the ones receiving no payment, gave blood. In the second group only 30 percent did. Offering to pay reduced the blood collected by nearly half.

Giving blood is an altruistic act, and the act of paying for that altruism (i.e., providing an extrinsic motivator) crowds out the intrinsic desire to do something good.

No wonder the Red Cross message "Giving blood provides a feeling money can't buy" works so well.

Retention Barrier 5: Chasing the unicorn

There's no better way to build high-commitment, high-value donors than to take steps at the acquisition stage to assure you're attracting the highest-quality donors. Before I offer suggestions on how best to improve the quality of your incoming donors, here are some thoughts on what to avoid.

What Not to Do

Many organizations—especially in this age of social media are obsessed with chasing the types of donors they don't have. Almost always the younger, more engaged, wealthy, and active variety. Anything but what they imagine their current donors to be—staid, not with it 50 to 70-year-olds.

More often than not this fixation serves as the rationale for seeking out a brand expert. He or she will help figure out what look, feel, message will best appeal to this imaginary group.

These new ones are unicorns. Beautiful but mythical creatures. The organization is confusing the channel of communication with the content of the communication.

Even though 20-somethings or 30-somethings are unlikely to respond to direct mail the way sixty- or seventy-year-olds do, the basic characteristics of committed donors don't depend on age.

What to Do

Thanks to inexpensive data analytics, cooperative data banks, and the willingness of groups to exchange lists, most organizations have access to lists of look-alike donors.

This is currently the standard practice for most organizations' acquisition programs—particularly groups dependent on direct response.

But is it the best practice when it comes to recruiting high-value, high-commitment, high-retention donors? Probably not, because many organizations withhold their choice donors from these data banks.

A better, more valuable approach is to build a profile of your organization's high-commitment, high-value donors and use that profile as a screen, filter, or model for identifying potential new donors.

The profile I'm suggesting differs from the usual donor profile in that it differentiates the characteristics of lower-value donors from those of higher-value ones.

Ask your list broker or the owners of donor lists you deal with to:

"High-Value Donors"

- Eliminate the lapsed donors of other organizations.
- If possible, select prospects who have been donors to other organizations for two years or more.
- Request prospects who have contributed a minimum of $25 or more in single gifts to other organizations.
- Avoid donors acquired primarily with the use of premiums.

Because a request like this is somewhat out of the ordinary, the business-as-usual crowd will offer countless reasons why it can't or shouldn't be done.

Persist and you'll see the payoff.

PART 3

The New Methodology and How to Increase Retention

10

Why Is Donor Attitude
So Important?

Understanding how donors feel about your organization and what role they want you to play in their lives is the starting point for improving retention rates.

Until you understand how your actions affect the donor's feelings toward you, you'll be in a constant guessing game when it comes to plugging the holes in your retention bucket.

For nearly 30 years the commercial world has understood the importance of attitude and has spent literally billions of dollars in understanding how to drive customer attitudes toward greater loyalty and commitment.

The result? According to Bloomerang.co, the commercial world enjoys customer retention rates approaching 90 percent. The national average of nonprofit retention rates is only 41 percent.

Some would argue that if you remove commercial enterprises such as utilities and cable providers, the commercial retention rate is lower than 90 percent. What is important is that compared to the commercial world, nonprofits do a poor job of holding onto their donors.

Milkshake Mistakes

Among the many great insights in Clay Shirky's *Cognitive Surplus* (2010, Penguin), I came across one valuable lesson for those of us involved in fundraising, nonprofit market research, or strategy.

Shirky describes a research project conducted at McDonald's. The aim was to improve the company's milkshakes by learning which attributes could be changed to improve sales. As you would expect, researchers prepared questionnaires and polled random customers about the quality and characteristics of McDonald's milkshakes.

A typical outcome might have been a report with detailed analysis of customer preferences about sweetness, taste, flavors—with specific recommendations about changes to improve sales.

But one of the researchers adopted a completely different approach. He spent several days sitting in a McDonald's restaurant observing customers who purchased the product. He discovered something unexpected—many were buying milkshakes during breakfast hours.

He further noticed an unusual pattern. Most of these customers came in alone, generally ordered the milkshake and nothing else, and wanted it to go.

Setting out to understand this behavior, the researcher learned that these customers by and large were commuting to work alone. The McDonald's milkshake was serving as the breakfast meal they could consume while driving. Its attributes made it perfect for the role it was assigned—it was filling, somewhat nutritious, and consumed easily with one hand on the wheel.

Almost everyone else missed the unexpected use of the milkshake because they had focused on the product rather than the customer. They also missed it because they had preconceived notions of how and when a milkshake is consumed and certain fixed ideas about what constitutes a typical breakfast.

The role McDonald's had assigned the milkshake wasn't the role many customers assigned to it. As Shirky points out about the researchers:

"They made two kinds of mistakes, things we might call 'milkshake mistakes.' The first was to concentrate mainly on the product and assume that everything important about it was somehow implicit in its attributes, without regard to what role the customers wanted it to play—the job they were hiring the milkshake for.

"The second mistake was to adopt a narrow view of the type of food people have always eaten in the morning, as if all habits were deeply rooted traditions instead of accumulated accidents. Neither the shake itself nor the history of breakfast mattered as much as customers needing food to do a nontraditional job—serve as sustenance and amusement for their morning commute—for which they hired the milkshake."

There are valuable lessons and insights here not only for fast food chains but for your organization as well.

First, a cause or an organization cannot be viewed apart from the market it serves. It is defined not only by its intrinsic features but also by the people (including donors) it serves.

Second, the organizational insiders' vision of the mission or brand may not always coincide with that of the donors. You may believe your organization does ABC, but your donors may contribute—and continue to contribute—because they believe it does XYZ.

I can't emphasize enough how important it is that an organization connect with its donors' values and beliefs. The path to poor performance is paved with trying to force your organization's perception of itself onto donors.

A principal reason that often motivates nonprofits to re-brand is their sense that "donors don't get us." As a result a brand consultant is hired, and countless dollars and loads of time are wasted. In *The Fundraiser's Guide to Irresistible Communications*, Jeff Brooks accurately describes the effort: "So, a brand is cooked up that will set those donors straight: Touche' you ignorant persons! This is what we are about! Love us now! That's the kind of brand that is deeply in trouble from the start. It's going to cost you dearly to educate those donors. And you'll fail to educate them."

The milkshake mistake here is believing you can win people over by trying to change their core beliefs and values. Try that and they'll leave you. Conversely, match the description of your organization with what they know and believe about it, and you'll keep them.

What Job Are Your Donors Hiring You to Do?

The loss of donors is silent and deadly. There's no screaming or shouting. No door slamming. Seldom any advance notice. One day they're just gone.

To make matters worse, many donors don't even realize they've stopped giving (remember from chapter 4 that 9 percent of all donors never remember supporting a particular organization in the first place). In their minds—and wallets—they've simply substituted another group for your organization.

This is why it's so important to discover, before the donor quits, which of the experiences you're providing are seen as positive or negative. Or to put it another way, to improve your retention rate, you have to understand what job the donor is hiring you for. Often you'll find that donors may value your organization for reasons you least expect.

Look around at the information, communications, and other experiences you serve up, and you'll find plenty of milkshake mistakes. You may think your donors give because they want the magazine, or because you have ten regional offices, or because your CEO appears in the *New York Times*. While important to organizational insiders, these characteristics may be of little interest to your donors.

And it won't help to infer attitude by segmenting your donor base by demographics (age, gender, education, income) or by past giving behavior (recency, frequency, monetary value).

Sure, if your donor is forty-two years old with a college degree and year after year has given to the year-end appeals on climate change, his or her demographic profile and previous giving *may be correlated* with that year-end giving decision, *but it didn't cause it.*

The key retention question that subconsciously resides in every donor's mind—and it doesn't involve demographic characteristics, is this: *How does this organization best enable me to make the difference I want to make?*

11

What Experiences Really Matter to the Best Donors?

L et's face it. At most organizations accurately identifying which experiences, among the dozens offered, truly matter to donors is a shot in the dark—akin to picking stocks by throwing darts at the NASDAQ listings in *The Wall Street Journal*.

You attend a conference and one speaker proclaims thank-yous matter most. Another insists it's really high-quality magazines and newsletters that count. You hear from another that sending too many appeals drives donors away.

And, of course, everyone in your organization has his or her own opinion and will justify and defend it rigorously.

In reality, as I outline in Part 4, chapters 15–19, there are actions— I call them key drivers of commitment—that really matter to donors, actions that don't matter at all, and some that are counterproductive and drive donors away.

Two Choices for Identifying Key Donor Experiences

As for identifying good, bad, or indifferent donor experiences, you have two choices, depending on how much time and effort you choose to put into the process:

1. You can simply build your retention plan using the generic or generalized seven key drivers identified in chapter 16, or . . . .
2. You can conduct a more detailed survey and analysis, custom-tailored to your organization, and apply the results as illustrated in chapter 13.

A note on surveying and measuring commitment:

That the world of survey research is replete with bad examples doesn't undermine the truism of proper surveying methodology being the *only* way to determine key experiences and measure commitment.

Suffice to say answers to survey questions alone don't give you a comprehensive understanding, much as donor behavior or transactional data don't provide a complete picture. The former, for example, is the only way to truly discern the *why* of motive, needs, and preferences.

In order to keep this book as brief as possible, the details of the survey methodology I'm proposing are set forth in the "Survey" section of the website at www.retentionfundraising.com. That said, it is important to point out all the survey findings and associated commentary in this book are based on analysis that *combines* attitudinal data with the transactional (giving) data of the donor in order to determine *cause* (donor experiences) and *effect* (donor behavior).

Why Donors Leave

Whichever approach you elect to follow, the objective is the same:

1. To identify the most likely reasons donors leave your organization, as illustrated below,

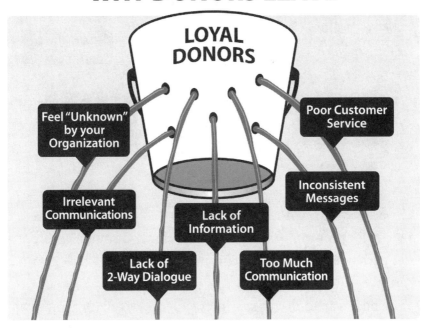

WHY DONORS LEAVE

LOYAL DONORS

Feel "Unknown" by your Organization

Poor Customer Service

Irrelevant Communications

Inconsistent Messages

Lack of Information

Lack of 2-Way Dialogue

Too Much Communication

and then.

2. Plug the holes by making the changes required to hold onto your donors:

ACTIONS TO KEEP YOUR DONORS

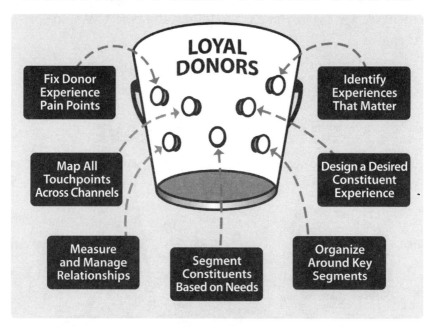

In order to draw the most effective and efficient road map to higher retention and greater donor value, you need to identify the experiences that deepen commitment and those that impact negatively.

The best way to discover which experiences matter and which don't is to ask. And the best way to ask the donor is with a survey tailored to your organization.

As illustrated below a survey of your donors will yield a list of key experiences.

IDENTIFYING THE KEY EXPERIENCES THAT MATTER

Donor Services

- Sending electronic receipts for donations
- Accurately fulfilling your request to update your contact information or donation preferences
- Providing helpful telephone/email/written service and support
- Providing knowledgeable telephone/email written service and support
- Resolving issues on first contact
- Calling donors to personally thank them

Engagement

- Take on advocacy action
- Organize an event
- Newsletter (quality, quantity)
- Publications (quality, selection, value)

Fundraising

- Online video (quality, quantity)
- Online giving (quality, ease of process)
- Tribute gifts
- Direct Mail (quality, quantity)

Brand

- Trustworthy
- Accountable
- Collaborative
- Creative
- Professional

Program

- Responding to international emergencies
- Building a better food system
- Right to know about impact of natural resource extraction
- Improving the way US delivers foreign aid

Key Messages

- Creating lasting solutions to poverty
- Creating lasting solutions to hunger
- Creating lasting solutions to injustice
- Helping communitites realize individualized solutions to their problems

Once you've identified these experiences, you'll know which you should continue (or even increase), which to reprioritize, and which to repair.

Best of all, you'll add big money to your bottom line and, in all probability, end up spending less as you dispense with activities that simply don't matter when it comes to donor retention and value.

APPLYING COMMITMENT MODEL TO CUT COSTS

The illustration above, from an actual case history, shows the savings that resulted from discovering what donors wanted—without jeopardizing their commitment level:

Until you determine specifically which experiences really matter to your donors, your retention efforts are likely to amount to little more than shots in the dark.

12

Identifying the Most Committed Donors

B uilding the most effective and efficient road map to higher retention and greater donor value requires two steps:

> *Step 1:* **Identifying the most and least committed donors,
> and . . .**
>
> *Step 2:* **Identifying the experiences that lead to or detract from
> high levels of commitment.**

With just these two insights you can reinforce or increase activities that enhance commitment while also repairing or eliminating
activities that damage it.

Let's turn first to the process of identifying your "best" or most
committed donors.

In chapters 7 and 8 we saw that key experiences will improve
donor retention. Now let's take a look at how you can establish a

benchmark for how committed your donors are. We'll call it a donor commitment score.

When you know the level of your donors' commitment, you'll be better able to manage your relationship activities by investing more time and money in the most highly committed donors and less in those less committed.

Unlike transactional behavior such as recency, frequency of giving, or monetary value (RFM), the donor commitment score is future oriented and far more accurate in projecting future performance and retention.

What's great is that out of hundreds of possible inquiries to determine the level of commitment, just the responses to three statements are all that's required to yield a donor commitment score:

"I am a committed (insert your organization name) donor"

"I feel a sense of loyalty to (insert your organization name)"

"(Insert your organization name) is my favorite charitable organization"

This is how the questions appear on a survey:

"SURVEY SAYS!"

7. On a scale of 0 to 10, please indicate how much you agree with each statement with "10" being "strongly agree" and "0" being "strongly disagree"

	Strongly Disagree	1	2	3	4	5	6	7	8	9	Strongly Agree
I am a committed (organization name here) donor	○	○	○	○	○	✓	○	○	○	○	○
I feel a sense of loyalty to (organization name here)	○	○	○	○	○	○	✓	○	○	○	○
(organization name here) is my favorite charity	○	○	○	○	✓	○	○	○	○	○	○

How to Calculate a Donor's Commitment Score

The donor commitment score is calculated using an unweighted average of the three responses. The highest possible score is a 10 ("strongly agree" for all three questions.)

Using the survey responses in the illustration above, the commitment score for this donor is a 6 (6 + 7 + 5 = 18 divided by 3 = 6).

Important note: a donor's response to any single question is irrelevant. Only the composite score matters.

I'm happy to report that this same technique for measuring the commitment level of an individual also works in determining the commitment level of your entire donor base.

Using this system you'll be able to identify:

High-commitment donors (scores in the 8–10 range). Those with the highest potential lifetime value and on whom you should concentrate most of your dollars and diligence.

Mid-commitment donors (scores in the 5–7 range). Those who fall midway on the commitment scale. These donors also warrant substantial attention, because with proper treatment they're likely to move to the high-commitment, high-value tier.

Low-commitment donors (scores under 5). Those who are most likely headed for the exit. If you have sufficient funds and time left over after attending to the top two tiers, you might turn your attention to these donors. But remember, even though low-commitment donors might be yielding a healthy return, by spending more money on donors at the high- and mid-commitment levels, you'll be making nearly four times more on your marketing investment.

What do you have to gain by conducting this survey? A lot.

National surveys conducted by DonorVoice of donors to 250-plus organizations in the United States, Canada, and the United Kingdom show on average that high-commitment donors yield 131 percent more revenue than low-commitment donors over a three-year period.

The table below shows the results from a direct mail appeal to high- and low-commitment donors on a house file. Note the enormous differential in return on investment between the high and low segments.

APPLYING COMMITMENT MODEL TO BETTER TARGET MARKET SPEND

Donor Voice Client Trust Results	High Commitment	Low Commitment
Response Rate	31%	13%
Average Gift	$22.06	$20.03
ROI	943%	229%

With this benchmark established, let's next turn next to actions you can take to begin increasing commitment and lifetime value.

Note: You can find a host of tools and resources related to donor commitment scores at www.retentionfundraising.com.

13

Putting the Survey Results to Work

You can apply the insights from a donor commitment survey in three highly meaningful ways:

Resource allocation. Shifting time and spending away from experiences and activities that are inconsequential. For example, you may find your organization's expensive magazine really doesn't matter to your donors, or that their eyes glaze over when being informed you have ten regional offices or are the largest organization in your sector.

Optimizing the experience. After identifying experiences that do matter, you want to offer them in the best way you can. For example, you may find that improvements in your thank-you and welcoming processes lead to higher commitment.

Targeting. Commitment scores, whether collected on a survey or through questions on all other communications (online, offline), can be used to better focus time and money on those donors most likely to be responsive—the highly committed.

Here's a fictional illustration of how the process works:

Like most organizations, the Good Deeds Charity is finding it difficult to grow net revenue year over year. The cost of acquiring donors has risen, and holding onto both new and older donors has proven problematic.

Good Deeds realizes it needs to improve its retention rate but doesn't know what actions it should take.

Development officer Jane Jones gathers the people responsible for communications, marketing, programs, and donor services and explains, "We need to measure our donors' level of commitment and find out what we're doing that pleases or displeases them—especially our most committed donors.

"We also need to determine which activities we're spending money on that don't matter."

Jane explains that the commitment survey is designed to measure how Good Deeds compares in donors' eyes to its competitors, what the overall level of donor commitment or loyalty is, and what actions Good Deeds is taking that matter or don't matter.

Jane's hunch is that the (expensive) annual report currently sent to everyone probably doesn't make much difference. This observation sparks a spirited discussion about other experiences the organization offers its donors.

Some express the belief that the thank-you or acknowledgment process is too slow. Others claim the organization asks for money too frequently and doesn't do a good job providing evidence of its success. Still others are convinced that by offering T-shirts and tote bags the organization "cheapens itself."

The group narrows down what they consider to be the key experiences they're offering to donors and includes them in the commitment survey.

The survey is e-mailed to all segments of the donor database. Soon the results come in and are tabulated.

Jane finds that donors with high commitment scores yield 217 percent more revenue than low-commitment donors.

For the high-commitment donors, the key experiences are:

1. Proper thank-yous expressing genuine appreciation,
2. Ability to reach the donor service line in the evening, and
3. Real-life stories about the people who benefit from Good Deeds, especially the program aimed at children.

Jane also discovers her hunch about the annual report is correct. Donors—whether high- or low-commitment—don't care about it.

Jane gathers her group again to review the results. Eyes are opened. A discussion ensues, and the following decisions are made: Eliminating the annual report will save $47,000.

Part of the savings can be used to improve the speed *and* content of the thank-you process, and another part can be earmarked to extending the hours and training of the donor service representatives.

In addition, it's clear from the commitment survey that other changes or tweaks in the communication and appeals schedule could be made at little or no cost.

Most important, substantial cost savings and far greater income can be realized if Good Deeds concentrates the best, but most expensive, experiences on the high-commitment donors.

Note: On the Retention Fundraising website (www.retention-fundraising.com), you'll find detailed information on a retention tool kit prepared by the DonorVoice team.

It's called Commitment-in-a-Box and includes:

- A template for the commitment survey, complete with a purpose statement for each section, programming notes if done online, and comments for preparing a printed version.
- An Excel workbook for the best ways to use the data from the survey to build relationships.
- A PowerPoint showing how to present and discuss your survey findings and how to apply them to drive change in your organization.
- A retention revenue forecaster to project the financial return that comes from increasing commitment on your donor file.
- A survey design best practices guide with how-tos should you elect to add additional questions to the survey template.

14

Plan Your Retention Changes

As a young man starting in fundraising, I was blessed with a seasoned and wise mentor by the name of G. Richard Kuch. He was a master at designing and managing large capital campaigns—undertakings that require meticulous planning and execution.

To this day, fifty-plus years later, his constant reminder of the importance of planning rings in my ears. "Craver, it's fine to believe in miracles, but it sure helps to organize for them."

All of which is to emphasize that reaching high commitment and retention levels among your donors simply won't happen without a plan and schedule.

Here's the four-step plan I use and recommend.

Step 1:
Identify the area of donor experiences on which you want to focus.

If you followed the commitment survey process outlined in chapter 12 and 13, you will have already identified one or more key donor experiences that need your attention.

Let's assume that one of the changes you need to make involves donor services.

Step 2:

Pinpoint those customer service or donor service experiences (different organizations assign different names to this function) identified by high-commitment donors as important and determine whether they are performing well or not.

It is this list of experiences that will form the basis for your change plan.

For ease of illustration, take a look at how the results from a typical survey can be arrayed to easily identify what changes are needed.

KEY EXPERIENCES FROM CUSTOMER SERVICE

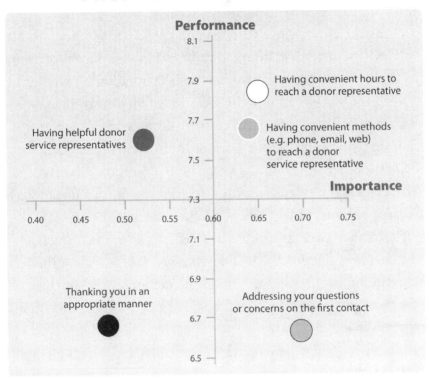

The goal with this chart is to provide a detailed road map for what to *focus on* and what to *change* for each category of experiences.

By plotting the importance *and* performance of the individual experiences for a given category, you can identify the activities that are:

High Importance and High Performance (upper-right quadrant)

High Importance and Low Performance (lower-right quadrant)

High Performance and Low Importance (upperleft quadrant)

Low Performance and Low Importance (lowerleft quadrant)

Using the chart above you can quickly see that:

"Having convenient hours to reach a donor service representative" and "Having convenient methods (phone, mail, written) to
reach a donor service representative" are both highly important and
performing well according to the organization's donors (upper-right
quadrant). Not much repair work or improvement needed here.

On the other hand, donors assign high importance but are seeing
poor performance when it comes to "addressing your questions or
concerns on first contact" (lower-right quadrant).

Here's an area crying out to be fixed, a hole in the leaky bucket.

If this organization has to cut its budget, save time, or otherwise
reallocate resources, the survey results demonstrated in the chart
show these cuts can be made in the area of acknowledgments/thank-
yous (lower-left quadrant).

Interestingly, the donor service department receives good marks.
Its staff simply needs to be taught how to answer questions and
concerns at first contact.

Note: On the Retention Fundraising website (www.retentionfun-
draising.com) in the section titled "Commitment-in-a-Box," you'll
find detailed information on a tool kit prepared by the DonorVoice
team. It includes a template Excel workbook that includes a section
to plot the experience chart illustrated above.

Step 3:

Focus on the experiences that need replacing, repairing, or deserve to be scaled or expanded, and place each in the proper category.

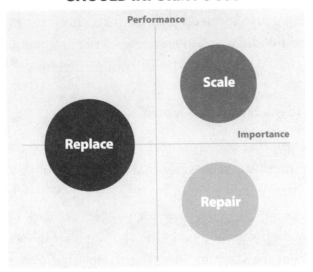

As seen in the illustration above, it's often useful to convey the actions that should be taken based on where experiences fall on the chart.

Questions to ask regarding "scale"

Is there a way to better deliver this key experience? For example, in the upper-left quadrant of the customer service chart on p. 75, "Having helpful donor service representation" gets a "high performance" rating but is of "low importance to donors." Doesn't look like any additional investment needs to be made to improve this function, because it's unlikely to affect commitment.

On the other hand, the upper-right quadrant shows that both "having convenient hours to reach a donor service representative" and "having convenient methods for reaching a donor service representative" are of high importance to donors. And because these functions have also received high performance ratings, the organization should take steps to ensure they're continually refined or increased, since doing so will boost commitment.

Questions to ask regarding "repair"

How do we improve performance? For example, in the lower-right quadrant of the customer service chart above, the "ability to address donors' questions or concerns on first contact" is of high importance to the donors. But in terms of performance it receives a low rating. The organization should look at the staffing level in its call center, the equipment it uses, and any other factor that may be slowing down response time in answering donor calls and inquiries.

Questions to ask regarding "replace"

What is the time and cost associated with this experience? Are there other reasons to keep it? For example, in the lower-left quadrant of the chart above, the function of "thanking you in an appropriate manner" is rated by donors as both low in importance and low in performance.

In this case the organization should be asking itself, "What are the implications if we simplify our complex and expensive acknowledgment process? How can we better use the time and money associated with this experience?"

Step 4:
Create a change plan for each category of experience.

By analyzing the way donors rate their experiences with your organization, you can ask yourself, "What changes can we come up with and then monitor? What additional answers do we need before we make a change?"

Answering these questions will allow you to create a change plan like the one illustrated below. You'll be able to review each category of experiences and reach agreement on the change, whether it is a near-term or long-term fix, and outline the immediate next steps.

KEY EXPERIENCE CHANGE PLAN

	Having convenient hours to reach a donor service represenative	Having convenient methods (phone, email, web) to reach a donor service represenative	Having helpful donor service represenatives	Addressing your questions or concerns on the first contact
Scale/ Repair/ Drop				
What is the change?				
Is this a near term change or long term change?				
Next steps?				

This isn't an easy process—positive change never is—but it is absolutely worth the effort.

PART 4

What to Do—Best Practices

15

Identifying Donor Experiences That Drive Commitment

As I see it, *the* fundamental flaw in our conventional fundraising belief system is this: "Donors are born, not made."

Those who believe this are convinced that if only they find the right data overlays, the right predictive acquisition models, or hit upon the right mailing lists and magic message, there's an enormous reservoir of new donors that'll come their way.

Countless millions are futilely spent trying to break the supposed code.

Fortunately, there's a more accurate and actionable approach to take if you really want to improve commitment, retention, and donor lifetime value.

We highlighted in earlier chapters the importance of establishing the proper relationship dynamics (i.e., reliability, consistency, fidelity, trust)—the so-called functional and personal connections that cause commitment.

That's only part of the equation, however. What is equally important is identifying the range of organizational actions required to *make* a good donor, especially those driving the donor toward greater commitment.

We call these essential activities *drivers*.

Identifying Key Drivers of Donor Commitment

In the DonorVoice study of 250-plus organizations, donors were asked to rate 32 drivers in terms of importance to them. The 32 drivers were:

Personal Connection Drivers  *(Emotion)*

1. Timeliness of the organization thanking me for my support
2. Sending a personalized thank-you for my support
3. Thanking me for my support in a way that makes me feel good about my donation
4. How regularly the organization thanks me for any ongoing support
5. Providing me with a feeling of accomplishment made possible by my support
6. Providing me with a feeling that my involvement is appreciated
7. Providing me with a feeling of being part of an important cause
8. Being an innovative charity
9. Being focused on the mission
10. Being a well-respected charity

11. Providing me with opportunities to take action for the cause [e.g., sign petition, organize others, attend rally]
12. Providing me with opportunities to get more involved [e.g., see the organization's work firsthand, meet staff, volunteer time]
13. Providing me with opportunities to make my views known [e.g., solicit my opinion on where effort should be focused, make it easy to make suggestions.]
14. Publicly recognizing my contribution

Functional Connection Drivers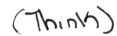

15. Informing me how my donation was used
16. Explaining the tax benefits of my donation
17. The organization's knowledge of the issues it focuses on
18. Efficiently spending money
19. Effectively trying to achieve its mission
20. Using donations ethically
21. Asking me for appropriate donation amounts
22. Keeping me informed about how the organization is getting results
23. Sending information that shows who is being helped
24. Sending information that makes me glad I support the organization
25. Sending information that reflects my specific interests
26. Providing readable information
27. The frequency of requests for donations
28. The frequency of information not requesting donations

29. Creating a sense in me that the organization would do a good job of responding to a complaint or question

30. Knowing what to expect from the organization each time it interacts with me

31. Communicating with me in the way I prefer [e.g., by mail, e-mail, phone, mobile device]

32. Having a similar look and feel to all communications with me.

That's a long if not unwieldy list, I realize, but we wanted to survey donors with as complete a list of options as possible.

So let's home in on the drivers and experiences donors found most important.

16

The 7 Key Drivers of Donor Commitment

From the master list of 32 possibilities, here are the 7 key drivers we've identified that most influence donors. They've been scored and ranked in order of their relative importance in improving loyalty, commitment, and value:

1. Donor perceives your organization to be effective in trying to achieve its mission. proof!
2. Donor knows what to expect from your organization with each interaction.
3. Donor receives timely thank-yous.
4. Donor receives opportunities to make his or her views known.
5. Donor is given the feeling that he or she is part of an important cause.
6. Donor feels his or her involvement is appreciated.
7. Donor receives information showing who is being helped.

Absent a study specifically focusing on your own organization, your retention efforts will be well served by placing your attention and efforts on these 7 key drivers.

You can begin immediately to improve your donors' experience and retention by determining how these 7 key drivers can be applied by your organization.

These drivers have a math-based, cause-and-effect relationship to loyalty and commitment. As you move donors from low to high commitment, the recency, frequency, and amount of their giving will rise dramatically.

I'll venture that one of the most powerful, productive—and fun—sessions you and the key players in your organization can have is discussing and brainstorming actions you can put in place to enhance each of the 7 key drivers and tailor them to your organization.

All that's required is an open mind, a pad of chart paper or a white board, and the creativity to adapt the drivers to your own organization.

17

Best Practices for Delivering on Key Drivers for *What* to Communicate

In this chapter, I'll focus on *what* to communicate when delivering on key drivers. In chapter 18, we'll turn our attention to *how* to communicate it.

Key Driver: Effectively trying to achieve mission

No one buys a Chevy because GM needs the money. By the same token, donors don't give because your organization has a need to balance its budget.

Although many think otherwise, donor expectations aren't usually driven by policy or programmatic details. Most often they're propelled by far more general and emotional factors: the need for donors to feel good about themselves . . . the warm glow that comes from supporting a cause or helping another person . . . a desire to advance justice, or end hunger, or even the wish to appear noble in the eyes of friends and peers.

Consequently, your job is to provide experiences and communications that reinforce these expectations—and in the process make donors feel an integral part of your group's success.

And please don't think it's your organization's name and logo that differentiate you. Rather, it's the collective set of impressions you provide that triggers and reinforces a donor's emotions and expectations.

These communications and experiences are what distinguish you from competing organizations. And they offer the best insurance you have that donors won't drift away.

How do you achieve this?

Let's start with two questions lurking in the back of every donor's mind: "Why do you need my money?" and "Did my contribution make a difference?"

You could answer these questions with facts, statistics, graphs, pie charts, policy papers, and slick annual reports. But if you do, you'll fail to make the essential personal or emotional connection you need.

Instead, answer with stories, photos, and videos about the youngsters you help, wildlife you save, refugees for whom you provide sanctuary, and the homeless you shelter—all thanks to the donor's help.

Master copywriter Jeff Brooks, whose *Fundraiser's Guide to Irresistible Communications* (Emerson & Church, 2013) belongs dog-eared on your desk, distills the recipe for a winning fundraising message into five simple rules:

1. You need a hero. (Your donor, not you!)

2. You need a goal. (Your donor wants to change the world and is looking for the right way to do so.)

3. You need an obstacle. (Make it clear there's a problem that needs solving.)

4. You need a mentor. (That's where you come in; you're the guide who makes it possible for the donor to change the world.)

5. You need a moral. (What's it all about? Don't assume everyone just knows.)

In my experience, the most overlooked and underutilized vehicle for conveying stories and the vitality of your organization's mission is the simple four-page newsletter.

Take a look at the example from Gillette Children's Specialty Healthcare in St. Paul, Minnesota. You can find dozens more illustrations like this in Tom Ahern's marvelous guide *Making Money with Donor Newsletters* (Emerson & Church, 2013).

Note the use of the story about "Zawandi" right on the front page . . . the photos of other beneficiaries on the top banner . . . and the list of other success stories on the left-hand panel with the headline "Because of You."

Gillette Children's
Specialty Healthcare
A CHILDREN'S MIRACLE
NETWORK AFFILIATE

Bringing You Closer to
the Lives You Help Change

Connections

Fall 2008 • Volume 1 • Number 1

Zawadi Says, "Thank You!"

You Helped a Tanzanian Girl Stand Tall on Her Own Two Feet

To meet Zawadi Rajabu, 6, is to experience gratitude through the eyes of a child. She greets you with a warm hug, a bright smile, and an emphatic, "Thank you!" Before you can grasp why you deserve such adoration, you catch a mischievous glint in her eye. "No catch me!" she taunts, running in the opposite direction. Another game of tag has begun, and — just like that — *you're it.*

It's an idyllic scene, but Zawadi's story doesn't begin here. Before she could even dream of chasing about in sparkly sneakers, Zawadi needed feet on which to stand.

Her Community Believed She Was Cursed
Zawadi was born with two clubfeet in an impoverished village outside Arusha, Tanzania. Her community saw the disability as a curse, and local children threw stones at her.

Zawadi's father abandoned the family the day she was born, leaving her mother to care for three children alone. "Zawadi would have no future if something happened to me," says Zawadi's mother, Sofia, through an interpreter.

Few Could Help Her
Zawadi's fate changed when missionaries Tom and Polly Wiley spotted her. "She had huge brown eyes and a penetrating look," Tom Wiley recalls. "We knew we had to help her."

The Wileys discovered that Zawadi's case was too severe for treatment in Tanzania. She needed a surgeon trained in the Ilizarov method — a complex technique for reshaping bones, developed by Gavriil Ilizarov, M.D., in a remote Siberian hospital. It was a tall order, to be sure.

But a Google search quickly uncovered one of the few surgeons in the world who could help Zawadi: Mark Dahl, M.D., pediatric orthopaedic surgeon at Gillette Children's Specialty Healthcare. In fact, Dahl trained in Siberia with Ilizarov himself.

"My Daughter Has a Future!"
Within weeks, Zawadi flew to St. Paul for a treatment that Dahl had performed thousands of times, but on only a few children with Zawadi's condition. During a five-hour surgery, Dahl

Zawadi continued on Page 4

Without treatment in Tanzania, Zawadi (right) learned to walk on the rough calluses that formed where her feet should be.

But today, Zawadi (above) is shopping for her first pairs of shoes! Wal-Mart helped her find shoes that fit around her braces, which will keep her feet straight while she grows.

Because of You!

Zawadi wears sparkly new shoes
Page 1

Douglas can visit an imaging center without crying
Page 2

Katie's memory continues to inspire
Page 2

Grace can say, "I love you!"
Page 3

A Word From Our President . . .
Margaret Perryman

What's So Special About
Specialty Care?

"Specialty health care" is a phrase we often use at Gillette, but what does it really mean? You might say that we focus on the hard stuff — some of the most uncommon diagnoses and complex treatments in medicine. Just read the real-life stories in this issue of *Connections*, and I think you'll understand what's so special about the care we provide.

For example: Who has one of the world's few surgeons skilled in the rare orthopaedic treatments pioneered by Gavrill Ilizarov in Siberia? We do.

Who has the technology to help a child break free from silence, expressing something as simple as, "I'm thirsty," or as profound as, "I love you"? We do.

Who has the vision to build new and innovative services, when it becomes clear that other options in the community are woefully inadequate? We do.

And who makes it all possible? You do.

Like all things rare and precious, specialty care for children at the margins of modern medicine is expensive. And because nearly half of our patients rely on Medicaid — a program that falls far short of reimbursing costs — we face a financial gap that only generous friends like you can fill.

It should come as no surprise that, without you, Zawadi might never have donned her first pair of shoes. Without you, Grace might never have told her mom that her favorite color is red. And without you, kids might never have had on-site imaging tests without pain and fear.

The truth is that you're among an exceptional group of people committed to ensuring that all children receive the best that medicine and technology can provide — regardless of the complexity of their disabilities or the financial resources at their command.

We do a lot of special things at Gillette. Perhaps the most important, though, is to say, "Thank you" to people like you, who make it all possible.

Thank you.

Why We Give
Our Children Inspired Us!

The Duvalls and the Kennedys knew what Gillette's Advanced Imaging Center would mean to children who have disabilities. In fact, their own children inspired them to help make the new center a reality.

We Wanted Douglas to Feel Safe

"I want people to know that their gifts matter to children like my son." Douglas Duvall, 9, used to cry at the mere sight of a radiology suite. Douglas requires a special tube to deliver medicines and nutrition into his small intestine. Before having surgery to place the tube permanently, Douglas frequently endured invasive X-ray procedures. At the time, Gillette didn't have advanced imaging services. "At other facilities, every visit was traumatizing," says Douglas' mom, Heather Duvall. "But without his medicines, Douglas would have seizures."

When Duvall learned that Gillette planned to build an Advanced Imaging Center, she immediately made a donation. Upon touring the new center, she learned about Gillette's positive-distraction technology, which comforts children with music, lighting and video images. "Douglas never cried during our visit!" she says. "I want people to know that their gifts matter to children like my son."

We Honored Our Daughter, Katie

Within hours of her birth in 1995, Katie Kennedy was diagnosed with microcephaly. A stroke before birth caused the condition, which results in significant neurological impairments. Given Katie's medical challenges and limited life expectancy, parents **"An on-site center is an amazing gift."** Kevin and Cindy Kennedy created The Sunshine Foundation to serve as her legacy. "The song, *You Are My Sunshine*, made Katie smile even during the most difficult hospitalizations," says Cindy Kennedy.

Katie died in February 2006, surrounded by her family. The Sunshine Foundation recently gave $17,000 to support Gillette's Advanced Imaging Center. "Traveling to off-site centers can be difficult for children and taxing for caretakers," Kennedy says. "An on-site center is an amazing gift. We hope our donation inspires others to give."

Tell Us Your Story!
What inspires you to support children who have disabilities? Please e-mail us at foundation@gillettechildrens.com. We might share your story in *Connections*.

We Need Your Help Today! Thanks to friends like you, our Advanced Imaging Center is meeting a vital need. But we still need to raise more than $3 million for the new center. To ensure that kids continue to have on-site imaging tests without fear, we invite you to make a gift today.

2

Make the Connection! Make a Difference

When you support Gillette, you provide world-class medical care for children who have disabilities. And showing your support has never been easier!

What You Can Do Today

- Sign up for our e-newsletter at www.gillettechildrens.org/newsletter.
- Donate today at www.gillette childrens.org/donate.
- Become a Guardian Angel monthly supporter by visiting www.gillettechildrens.org/guardianangels.
- Ask your employer to match gifts you make to Gillette. To see if your employer already matches gifts, visit www.matchinggifts.com/gillettechildrens.
- Recycle electronics at gillette.myboneyard.com, and the value of your used electronics will be donated to Gillette.

Just in Time for the Holidays!

Supporting Gillette is as easy as shopping for holiday gifts!

- Find the perfect gift at www.giftback.com/gillette, and 10 percent of every purchase is donated to Gillette.
- Better yet, make your purchases with a Gillette credit card. Sign up at www.gillettechildrens.org/creditcard. Gillette receives $50 the first time you use your card and 0.3 percent of every purchase made — all at no additional cost to you!

Connections is a quarterly publication of Gillette Children's Specialty Healthcare. Direct comments and questions to Andrew Olsen at 651-229-1766 or foundation@gillettechildrens.com.

4

Thank You Wal-Mart!

Zawadi Loves Her New Shoes

Wal-Mart in Maple Grove — a Children's Miracle Network sponsor — couldn't let Zawadi return to Tanzania without some new shoes. When store co-manager Mike Peckis presented a pair with pink sparkles, Zawadi's eyes lit up. "Yes!" she exclaimed. Peckis (pictured here with Zawadi and shoe department manager Joann Hogan) was just as enthusiastic. "I have goose bumps," he says. "The spirit of the kids we help is phenomenal."

Zawadi continued from Page 1

attached steel rings with struts, called fixators, to the bones in her feet and legs. Zawadi's mother then tightened the struts several times a day, slowly reshaping Zawadi's feet.

After two months of sometimes painful daily adjustments, Zawadi's feet were straight. "I never dreamed she could walk like every other child," says Zawadi's mother. "My daughter has a future!"

You Reach the World — and Your Neighborhood

Zawadi returned to Tanzania in September — with a new lease on life that you made possible. By supporting Gillette, you're providing world-class medical treatment to children for whom Gillette might be the only option. So when Zawadi says, "Thank you," we couldn't agree more.

Thanks for a Great Day!

You Helped Families Facing Disabilities Forge New Connections

Thanks to these generous sponsors, Gillette children and families recently enjoyed a day at Como Zoo filled with food, fun, prizes and — best of all — new connections!

- Checkers
- Chipotle Mexican Grill
- Costco
- Dairy Queen
- Great Clips
- IHOP
- Marriott City Center
- Marriott Depot
- Miss Minnesota
- Muller Family Theatres
- Panda Express
- Speedway/SuperAmerica
- State Farm Agent Heather Brooks Stafani
- State Farm Agent Yvonne Peterson
- Strategic Fundraising, Inc.
- Tamarack Habilitation Technologies

A Special Thanks to

Momtalk.com

Meagher & Geer

- Trader Joe's
- TurnKey Direct Marketing
- Wal-Mart
- Wells Fargo Private Client Group

Help your donors feel they're an integral part of a collective experience by sharing testimonials from other donors and beneficiaries of your organization's work. Mix it up. Report on big wins and small wins. Just take a look at the Gillette example—lots of wins, all being made by ordinary people and donors as well as experts.

Key Driver: Making the donor feel he or she is part of an important cause

Out of the blue one day in my mailbox appears an envelope reading, "Office of the Probate Court" in that old-style Gothic type still used by parts of the American legal system. Thinking perhaps I was the unlikely heir to an unknown benefactor, I ripped it open.

My disappointment at inheriting nothing was quickly replaced with a joy that many donors like me were feeling that day. The letter was from an African American probate judge in Mississippi thanking me for contributing to the Southern Poverty Law Center.

The judge went on to explain that, thanks to the generosity of donors like me, the Southern Poverty Law Center had succeeded in breaking down one hundred-plus years of racial prejudice where the Mississippi judiciary was concerned and that he wanted me to know of his gratitude for my support of the Center.

Any donor who at that moment didn't feel proud to be part of this important cause probably couldn't read.

Not only was the letter from the probate judge one of the most powerful thank-yous I've ever received, it stands as a testament to the importance of conveying to donors their important role in advancing the mission of the organization.

Too many of our organizations believe that *importance* is conveyed by such superlatives as "we're the biggest" . . . "we have twenty regional offices" . . . "Our cost of fundraising is only 10 percent." In reality these statements are meaningless. No one outside the organization really cares. Certainly not donors.

What is important to donors is that you're getting results. Doing the job he or she hired your organization to do. Winning racial justice . . . curing disease . . . feeding kids.

There are any number of ways to illustrate your organization's accomplishments while reinforcing the donor's belief that he or she made a giving choice that truly mattered, and continues to matter.

Perhaps, as in the case of the Southern Poverty Law Center, you offer up a powerful third-party testimonial from someone who benefited from your organization's work. Or maybe you can gather a fistful of news clips reporting on your recent accomplishments and send them to the donor with a simple note: "I thought you'd like to see what your support just made possible."

Strong organizations keep their promises. This key driver serves as a reminder that you need to demonstrate in powerful and varied ways how your organization is keeping its word.

Key Driver: Sending information showing who is being helped

My hat is off to such organizations as Child Fund and Charity Water. Both have mastered the art of letting their donors know in moving, specific, and quite human terms how much their support means.

Rather than bog down donors in a swamp of global data on the plight of children, Child Fund sets aside statistics and piecharts and sends a hand-scrawled letter from the child they're helping in Ethiopia, a note from the grateful grandma in South Africa, or a video from the teacher or doctor amidst the hellish aftermath of war.

Charity Water is a master at making the complex simple and actionable. Look at this online year-end appeal thanking donors for their previous support while seeking a quite specific year-end contribution.

Change the lives of families in Cambodia this holiday season. Donate a filter and help bring clean water into more than 15,000 homes.

Note how Charity Water so quickly and concisely lets its donors know what's already been accomplished (1,634 campaigns already launched for Cambodia), what the goal of this effort is (15,385 more filters to fund), and what each donor's share is ($65 per filter.) No wonder this is one of the world's fastest-growing charities.

There are countless variations of what I call slice-of-life reporting that any organization with access to the Internet and a digital camera can use. All that's required is focus on the individuals being helped and that two-word sentence: "Thank you!"

18

Best Practices for Delivering on Key Drivers for *How* to Communicate

Let's now turn our attention to *how* best to communicate.

Key Driver: Knowing what to expect from the organization with each interaction

Consistency and reliability are essential pillars of strong relationships. If donors can rely on your organization to be responsive—whether *responsive* means updating a change of address, effectively answering an inquiry, or consistently stating your mission—you'll win their trust and loyalty. If you fail, you'll lose them. It's that simple.

Often it's the little things that lead to a breakdown of trust. Gifts that go unthanked. Requests for information that aren't heeded. A telephone call not answered promptly, or worse yet, dealt with by a rude or unknowledgeable representative.

How can you begin to know if your organization is building trust? You can take two simple steps immediately. First, mail in your own contribution and track the timing, consistency, and quality of the thank-you. Second, pick up the phone and call the number listed in the Contact Us section of your website. Is the response you receive from these two simple actions what you as a donor expect?

In addition, pay particular attention to complaints. Donors who care the most are often the ones who will take the time to express their concerns.

Here's an example of one organization that goes out of its way. Phyllis Freedman, veteran fundraiser and planned-giving expert, shares this personal experience as a gold-standard example.

Phyllis and her family had established an endowed scholarship to honor her late brother. Here's the letter she received from the University of Texas School of Architecture in response to some concerns she expressed:

Dear Ms. Freedman,

Recently, I attended my first graduation ceremony as the new Assistant Dean for Development in the School of Architecture, and it was a lovely and inspiring day. As Dean Fritz Steiner shared in his comments, our students have an amazing commitment to making a positive difference in the world, and their scholarship and academic achievement is first-rate.

I wanted to share the commencement program with you as all of our scholarships are listed, and I thought you might like to see the names of the Ted Freedman Endowed Scholarship recipients. As you can imagine, our scholarship recipients are among the best and brightest on campus, and support for these students makes a tremendous difference in their lives.

Ms. Freedman, I know that you have been understandably disappointed with the School of Architecture. I hope that you received my phone messages from earlier this spring expressing Dean Steiner's wish to meet with you during his most recent trip to Washington, D.C. If there is ever an opportunity in the future for Dean Steiner to visit with you, he would very much like to do so.

When and if you feel the time is right, please contact me, and we will schedule his trip accordingly. My card is enclosed for your reference, and I hope that we will have the chance to visit with you in the future.

Sincerely,

Julie M. Hooper

Julie M. Hooper, CFRE
Assistant Dean for Development

Thoughtfully accompanying the letter was a copy of the commencement program listing the scholarship in her brother's name.

Years later, the University of Texas continues to do things right. Recently, Phyllis sent me this update: "My mother, who established that fund in my brother's memory, passed away last month. I got a real sympathy card—not a letter on official letterhead—from the dean of the School of Architecture."

Key Driver: Timeliness of thank-yous

When it comes to acknowledging and thanking donors, an infinite amount of advice abounds in our sector. Some claim a highly personal thank-you is essential. Others argue that personal isn't nearly as important as getting something to the donor as quickly as possible.

In our studies, we've found donors themselves put a premium on timely thank-yous. A slight majority define *timely* as a note arriving within forty-eight hours, while the vast majority indicated they wanted their gift acknowledged no more than a week after it was received.

A caveat on timeliness: quick thank-yous have become more the norm or a so-called best practice today. They won't distinguish or differentiate you as much as they once did. As a result, I suggest you focus more on the acknowledgment aspect of the communication, stressing why the gift is appreciated, why it matters, and how it was put to work.

Because thanking donors is critical to retention, you'll likely need to make some changes and compromises within your organization. For example, if your policy is to have the CEO personalize and sign all the thank-yous and the stack is piling up on his or her desk, then you've probably placed your bet on the wrong horse.

Strategically and operationally, any organization sacrificing timeliness for personalization (and vice versa) should change course and figure out how to do both.

Here's an example from Ken Burnett that incorporates timeliness, a personal tone, and deals with the issue of cost should it arise in the donor's mind:

"Dear Mrs. _____,

"Thank you for your gift, which is already making a difference. Just so you know, it's our policy here at Panda Survival Trust to always acknowledge every donation, for three good reasons.

"1. So you can be sure your gift has been safely received and applied as you intended.

"2. Because we can use the opportunity to show you the impact your support has, the difference it makes to the welfare of pandas everywhere.

"3. And because we consider it not just basic politeness, but also one of our best, most mutually useful opportunities to connect with you, our valued supporter.

"From the last 27 years working with our supporters to help pandas, we've learned that when our donors—just like you—see the difference their support is making they find it very encouraging. When our donors are happy, that encourages them to continue their support. So you'll see, sending a simple thank you and brief update is neither costly nor a chore for us. On the contrary, we love to do it, and it's one of the very best investments we can make to ensure long-term support for the pandas from people like you.

"On behalf of all of us, thank you for your generous gifts. They're much appreciated, because they make possible everything we do.

"With best wishes . . .

"[Signature]"

Please go back and read the first sentence in Ken's letter: "Thank you for your gift, which is already making a difference." Too many of our acknowledgment letters don't go much further than the thought contained in that sentence. And that simply isn't good enough. Instead, the content that follows is the real meat of a proper acknowledgment and thank-you.

Recently Ken wrote me to add, "Whenever I talk about thanking donors nowadays I always suggest going further than just thanking, by *congratulating* the donor on doing something wonderful. This can be thrilling for them, of course, and also gets over the concern some donors feel (i.e. cancer survivors) that really they should be thanking us, for the opportunity to give to something that might save their life."

Key Driver: Providing opportunities to make views known

Seems like every day I receive an online survey seeking my opinion of a service I've just used, whether an airline flight, a stay in a hotel, or a package that landed at my doorstep from Amazon.

Consumer companies spend billions seeking their customers' feedback. They know the mere act of asking for the customer's opinion—regardless of the answer or whether the individual even responds—will boost satisfaction and loyalty.

I wish the same were true for our nonprofit sector. But it's not.

The most significant demographic change in fundraising—the shift from the World War II generation of donors (those now in their 70s and 80s) to the younger generations of Baby Boomers and Generations X and Y—puts a premium on donor feedback.

Study after study by DonorVoice, DonorTrends, and dozens of other research companies confirm that younger generations are more skeptical and demand more involvement than the blindly loyal World War II generation of donors. They need to feel listened to.

Despite this, we often relate to our donors on an antediluvian communications path running one way—from the organization to the donor. We behave as if we have one mouth and no ears. Often we pontificate and tell donors what great organizations we are. We ask for money. We ask for more money. But we don't listen. And donors leave in droves.

Fortunately, today's inexpensive communications technologies offer boundless opportunities for organizations and donors to connect and interact.

The experience of People for the Ethical Treatment of Animals (PETA) is just one example of the power of the telephone town meeting or teleconference. Steve Kehrli, director of development of the PETA Foundation, reports that:

> PETA holds telephone town meetings not for fundraising per se, but to introduce donors to campaigns, to expose donors

to PETA's energetic and committed staff and to get donor questions and testimonials.

Donors who make larger gifts seem to love telephone town halls. These givers showed dramatic increases in subsequent giving from the mere fact they were invited, even if they didn't attend.

The meetings themselves boost response. Donors who listened to some or all of the meeting gave 60% more than those who only heard about it. And those who stayed on the meeting call for over 15 minutes donated 3.5 times more than those who only heard about it.

Steve believes that a mere invitation to these meetings, regardless of participation, is boosting overall retention rates.

A second communications tool that can boost donor commitment for less cost than a daily cup of coffee is the online survey. I'm thinking here of the type of survey that pops up when someone has taken action on your website, or one that is sent to a donor or prospect who's telephoned your call center to make an inquiry, change his or her address, or file a complaint.

There's a good reason these types of surveys are so ubiquitous in the commercial world—airlines, hotels, Amazon, you name it. They not only represent a low-cost way to build loyalty and retention, they're great for spotting and quickly resolving problems.

You'll find various tools and widgets listed at this book's website: www.RetentionFundraising.com.

Key Driver: Make the donor feel that his or her involvement is appreciated

Remember when you first fell in love? You were sure that exhilarating rush would last forever. Alas, as we all know, the early flames of a long-term relationship usually die down. A stable bond replaces the exhilaration. But that bond, too, needs occasional juicing if it's to stay healthy and deepen.

Donor relationships are no different. Keeping a healthy, fiery, and deepening connection takes effort.

In my experience there are three ways to keep the spark alive and forge a devoted, lasting connection between your organization and donors.

1. Know and experience your organization from the donor's perspective.

Most organizations work hard and spend a lot of time marketing their missions and their brands. But a wise fundraiser knows it's just as important to experience an organization's core behaviors, benefits, and experiences just as a donor does. This is really the only way to feel your organization's value and make sure it hasn't lost its way.

One simple technique is mystery shopping. Years ago Ken Burnett, in preparation for his book *Friends for Life: Relationship Fundraising in Practice* (White Lion Press, 1996), organized a series of tests in the United Kingdom, United States, Canada, and Australia to gauge the levels of donor service.

He sent a lovely letter from "Rebecca," a recent widow, to thirty U.S. organizations. Rebecca hinted she might eventually make a large gift (she did include a $5 bill as an indication of interest), but that she would like more information about the organization's work. She even included such tip-off phrases as "until my husband's estate is settled."

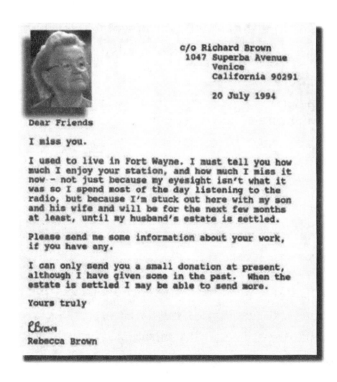

```
                                    c/o Richard Brown
                                    1047 Superba Avenue
                                    Venice
                                    California 90291

                                    20 July 1994

Dear Friends

I miss you.

I used to live in Fort Wayne. I must tell you how
much I enjoy your station, and how much I miss it
now - not just because my eyesight isn't what it
was so I spend most of the day listening to the
radio, but because I'm stuck out here with my son
and his wife and will be for the next few months
at least, until my husband's estate is settled.

Please send me some information about your work,
if you have any.

I can only send you a small donation at present,
although I have given some in the past. When the
estate is settled I may be able to send more.

Yours truly

RBrown
Rebecca Brown
```

The results? Disappointing to say the least.

Of the thirty groups Rebecca wrote to, only fourteen answered. Of those fourteen, most took three or four weeks to respond.

Rebecca received lots of irrelevant standard letters and forms. Only one organization used large type, although it was clear Agnes was an older lady. *Use large font for elderly*

An activity like mystery shopping—and mystery listening—can be eye-opening. Spend a few hours in the mail room opening correspondence and some nights or weekends on the phones in your organization's donor service center. See what questions donors are asking, become familiar with folks who handle the mail or who work the phones, and how they answer questions.

Another approach is to visit a project and let it subtly be known that you're a donor. Were you welcomed? Well received? Treated like a member of the family?

There are few investments in time worth more. You'll discover strengths and weaknesses you never knew your organization had.

2. Delight with novelty and surprise.

Almost every organization falls into routines. Changing things up and adding a little variety can boost your donors' commitment. Simone Joyaux calls these extraordinary experiences "memorable moments . . . their purpose is to delight the donor."

According to Simone, such moments can be as simple as an informal gathering at the office where you tell donors how you spend their money and invite their input. Or you might collect donors' philanthropic stories and share them on your website or in your newsletter. Or invite donors to tell their stories at events.

I wish I worked at a zoo, because my favorite suggestion from Simone is to invite donors to help feed the animals!

There are numerous ways to create extraordinary experiences, delight donors, engage their interest, and create surprise. As Simone preaches, "If you focus on these, rather than always focusing on raising more money, ironically the increased donor loyalty will result in more money."

3. Know when to listen and communicate—genuinely.

If you take the term *donor-centric* seriously, you'll uncover which of your donors' interests matter most and help them reach their aspirations through memorable moments, unique giving opportunities—even after the donor has stopped giving.

The Audubon Society of Rhode Island goes to a lot of time and trouble to show their donors how much they understand and care for them—including giving away free memberships to those who have stopped giving.

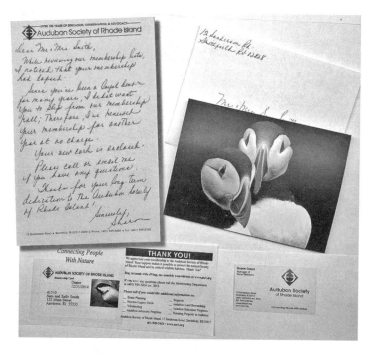

Audubon calls it a "Don't-worry-about-it" forgiveness program. Members who were with the society for ten-plus years but haven't renewed their memberships receive a special package.

It's possible the renewal has escaped your notice, the letter says, but even if the member chooses not to renew, the society knows he or she is committed to protecting birds and their habitat.

Given that it doesn't want the former member to miss out on important information, a new card is enclosed, and the donor's membership is extended for another year—for free.

Yes, free!

The result? Lapsed members began sending in their $45 dues, with some sending $100 or more. In fact, since Audubon began this effort, an impressive 50 percent of the lapsed members have renewed, with a whopping 50 percent making larger gifts than before they lapsed!

To its donors the Audubon Society of Rhode Island walks the walk: "You, dear member, are worth far more than your donation."

19

Easy Retention Wins for Everyone

My grandfather, a mathematics professor, used to speak to me like an expert, not a grandson. As a kid I'd ask him to help me solve some numbers problem for the next day in school. Before getting to the problem at hand, however, he felt he needed to explain the foundation of mathematics. Tedious and frustrating. This is probably why I became a consultant, anything but a mathematician.

What I did learn is that when you listen to an expert explain a problem, the first urge is to delegate it back: "Do it for me, Grandpa, it's too complicated."

Riding a bike for the first time is also complicated if you don't know how. But once you get the hang of it, the process becomes easier and easier. While it's best to learn to ride the retention bike by following the framework and process I've detailed in these pages, there are some universal dos and don'ts that'll move you forward even before you're an expert bike rider.

That's because, whether your organization is huge, tiny, or in between, there are a number of general or universal donor experiences that are relatively easy and inexpensive to fix. Doing so will immediately help boost your donor commitment and retention.

Retention Win 1: Say thank you

The art of saying thank you is one key to building great relationships. Unfortunately, it's often ignored. Many organizations take weeks, sometimes months to acknowledge gifts. Others never even get around to it.

Too many of us view acknowledgments (the term alone speaks volumes) with a jaundiced eye. We see them as a cost and a pain. As nonprofit communications expert Erica Mills puts it, "Acknowledging isn't thanking. An acknowledgment doesn't make the recipient feel warm and fuzzy about what they've done. It makes them remember that soon they'll have to file taxes. That's stressful, not joyful."

My files are filled with notes from fundraisers who know better. Angel Aloma at Food for the Poor writes:

Thank-you letters have been effective fundraisers for our organization. On average, we get more than one-fifth of our net income from them. We pay a lot of attention to the quality and strength of the letters and make sure they are tremendously donor centric. We don't include any ask in the letter, but we do include an envelope and a reply piece.

Amongst our highest donors, we tested two groups. At the beginning of the year we sent a sincere, simple thank you card to 25,000 donors for their past generosity—no ask, no reply piece, no envelope. The other group didn't receive this. Both groups gave almost identical *numbers* of gifts that year, but the group that received the thank-you gave almost $450,000 more.

Thank-yous are most effective when personal and relevant, as evidenced by this comment from fundraising consultant Jessica Harrington:

For one organization's first renewal, we personalized the letter to the year the donor first joined and what was happening then. For example, if the donor joined in 1980, she was supporting the organization's Call to Halt the Arms Race. Or if a donor joined in 2008, she was supporting the *Anniversary* counter-recruitment movement. We then showed key milestones the donor helped achieve since she first contributed.

We didn't just pull out a date or reference a package—the customization was several paragraphs long and took the donor through the organization's history and her involvement and recognized that none of this could have happened without her.

Of course, the key was linking the past accomplishments and donations to why her support was needed today.

We think we did that. Revenue is up 54%!

Helen Keller, the great American icon and leader of the movement to educate the blind, was also a great fundraiser who understood how to express gratitude.

Her thank-you letter to Alexander Graham Bell, who made it possible for Ms. Keller to give her beloved teacher, Anne Sullivan, a fine wedding present, shows clearly what I mean by personal and relevant.

Dear Mr. Bell,

I was perfectly delighted to get your letter, and I thank you ever so much for sharing with me the pleasure of giving Teacher a present. I should have written sooner, but the gift arrived only yesterday. I bought her a beautiful clock and candelabra that go with it, as I happened to know that was just what she wanted. I value a secret both for itself and for the exercise it gives my faculties to keep it, and I felt delightfully important and responsible when you put such a large secret into my hands! You know how hard it is to conceal anything from Teacher who is quite a clairvoyant, and I was quite proud when she told me that neither she nor Mr. Macy [the groom] suspected our secret . . . .

How beautiful the scene on the lawn must have been, and how fitting it was that her happiness should thus be blended with the glory of the blue sky and the fragrance of growing things! Teacher's marriage will take place Tuesday instead of Wednesday. There is a boat which leaves Wednesday, and she and Mr. Macy want to take it for a fine trip.

My mother is here, and I shall go home with her after the wedding and spend part of the summer with my other dear ones in the South.

With dear love to you and Mrs. Bell, I am,
Your affectionate friend,
Helen Keller

Certainly beats a computer-generated receipt or formulaic printed acknowledgment.

Resource note: do yourself and your organization a favor. Visit Lisa Sargent's Thank-you Letter Clinic at SOFII, the showcase of fundraising innovation and inspiration (http://www.sofii.org/article/ ✈ how-to-write-a-better-thank-you-letter-and-why-it-matters). There you'll find a treasure trove of how-to advice and thank-you letters you can swipe.

Retention Win 2: Improve your donor services

Although correcting some experiences involves a good deal of time, work, and internal debate, there's one retention mistake most organizations can easily fix—poor service.

Too often we treat donor service as an afterthought, assigning it to an unpaid intern to handle during lunchtime. We mistakenly treat it as a cost center, when in reality good donor service actually adds thousands, tens of thousands, or hundreds of thousands to the bottom line because of its positive effect on donors' attitudes.

From our studies, it's clear that virtually all organizations should be offering the following. Failing to do so costs the average organization about 20 percent of its donors:

- Convenient options for reaching donor service agents (e-mail, website, live chat, phone)
- Convenient hours of operation to reach a live operator or donor representative
- Helpful and knowledgeable customer service support

What does great donor service look like? Hopefully, it's as on the ball as this experience reported by fellow fundraiser Simone Joyaux:

> One of my most memorable (positive and wonderful) experiences—as a donor—involves a mistake made by EMILY's List, the pro-choice Democratic women's political action committee.
>
> I received a gracious email saying that my membership was expiring and EMILY would love me to renew. I called and said, "Gee, I think I did renew."
>
> First, I easily connected with the membership office. No voice mail hell. The membership person immediately found my record and apologized for the mistake. Off I went to a meeting. Returned to my office and an email awaited me, apologizing for the error. "That's nice," I thought. "Nice apology on the telephone when I called. Nice email follow-up apology."
>
> After traditional business hours, about 6 p.m., I get a telephone call from the senior development officer at EMILY's List. She apologizes again, explaining what had happened. (By the way, I received an explanation of what went wrong both in my original telephone chat, and in the email.)
>
> And then the senior development officer says to me: "I was looking at your record, Ms. Joyaux. And did you know that 3 days from today will be your 20th anniversary as an EMILY donor? We are so thrilled that you have been such a loyal donor. We hope you are thrilled and proud, too."

And I am thrilled and proud to be a loyal donor to EMILY's List. Wow. 20 years? I had no idea. And I am impressed at their quick response to a mistake. Everyone makes mistakes. No big deal. But they acknowledged and apologized for their mistake so well and so quickly and with extra attention and care and graciousness and . . . I sure enjoyed that dopamine high! I tell the story over and over.

Retention Win 3: Be boring

Most of us get bored with our organization's messages long before our donors do. So we're constantly fiddling with new copy, new creative, clever new ways to describe our mission and programs. Tinker. Tinker. Change. Change.

As a result we waste prodigious amounts of time and money on new creative. All this tinkering may relieve our boredom, but when we alter or deviate from our organization's core message, we risk confusing donors and driving them away.

There's a reason successful political candidates employ the same stump speech at every stop, boring the life out of their staff, themselves, and the traveling press corps: consistency.

There's a reason successful consumer companies err if they deviate from the makeup of their core product (think New Coke): consistency.

The same holds true for nonprofits that are successful year after year: consistency counts. A lot.

Be especially vigilant about consistency where new and first-year donors are concerned. A donor who makes his or her first gift because of a direct mail package featuring a powerful story on rescuing abused cats and dogs isn't as likely to make a second gift if thanked with a letter or e-mail touting the organization's work to save porpoises.

To ensure consistency, organizations regardless of size, need someone in charge of reviewing all communications—mail, e-mail, website, or phone.

Retention Win 4: Give donors lots of opportunities to talk back

All successful relationships—including those with donors—require the give and take of two-way communication.

Yet too many of us fail to seek feedback from our donors.

We seek their money—that's one form of feedback, of course. But so is soliciting their opinion. Why do so many organizations relegate feedback to a banal direct response tactic such as placing a survey on the reply form, or forcing the donor to hand-write a note on the same reply form, only to have it summarily tossed when it reaches the organization's mail room?

Every organization regardless of size or sophistication has dozens of opportunities to solicit feedback. Among them:

- Holding an inexpensive telephone town hall meeting to seek your donors' opinions.
- Sending a brief e-mail survey to your donors after every contact they have with your donor service center. Ask if their needs were met, if they're satisfied.
- Using e-mail or postal mail to determine your donors' level of loyalty or commitment. You can do this with the three simple commitment questions outlined in chapter 11.

- Installing a pop-up website survey to determine users' level of satisfaction in finding the information they seek.

Here's an interesting fact. Whether donors answer your survey positively or negatively—and even if they choose not to respond at all—the mere act of asking their opinion will help boost retention.

You can find a range of techniques and inexpensive feedback widgets at this book's website at www.retentionfundraising.com

Retention Win 5: Pick up the phone

I'm continually surprised at how little the telephone is used to bolster donor commitment and retention.

Other than a face-to-face meeting with your donors, there's nothing better than a phone conversation when it comes to listening, interacting, sharing values, and building trust.

Consider the advantages:

According to a study by the British telemarketing firm Pell & Bales, for every £100 spent on thank-you calls there is a return of £1,000.

And it's not just thank-you calls that work. Telephone calls inviting donors to join monthly giving programs (a good retention strategy in itself) can yield a ten times greater response rate than direct mail, according to studies by the U.S. analytics firm DonorTrends.

Overall, donors who have been phoned for one reason or another (it doesn't seem to matter) show retention rates 15 percent higher than those who haven't been contacted.

Just as in the case of seeking feedback through surveys, the mere act of phoning, regardless of whether the donor responds positively or negatively, boosts retention.

So, pick up the phone and call.

Retention Win 6: Monthly giving

One important but not-so-easy retention win should be on everyone's list: a robust monthly giving or sustainer program. It's the fundraising equivalent of going steady.

Chuck Longfield, chief scientist at Blackbaud, preaches a lot about retention and how monthly giving programs relate to it. If you can communicate with someone monthly and also receive a contribution every thirty days or so, he or she will be among your most loyal donors.

Chuck fervently believes sustainers are so important that he's labeled the imperative to enlist them as "fundraising's last land grab."

Although typical donors may give to five or even ten organizations a year, a monthly donor will usually limit her or his giving to two or maybe three groups. Thus, Chuck's admonition to get there first.

Unfortunately, few organizations in the United States seem to recognize the opportunity. The Canadians, Europeans, and now Asians are way ahead of U.S. nonprofits.

Why? Some excuse-prone fundraisers blame it on America's banking system. The U.S. equivalent of direct-debit elsewhere in the world is the more cumbersome Electronic Funds Transfer System or the old-fashioned credit card system.

But that's a pallid excuse. U.S. groups that have demonstrated skill and staying power—such as Greenpeace, the Southern Poverty Law Center, and ASPCA—are prospering with committed monthly donor programs.

As Harvey McKinnon in his classic *Hidden Gold* (Taylor Trade Publishing, 2003) alerted fundraisers a decade ago:

> "Monthly giving appeals not only to younger donors who find it convenient and easy, but also to older donors, who are more likely to live on a budget. But, regardless of their age monthly donors will often give for decades, are more loyal than even the most consistent annual donors and are far more likely to leave bequests."

And Erica Waasdorp in her book *Monthly Giving: The Sleeping Giant* (A Direct Solution, 2013) clearly illustrates the value of a monthly donor:

> "Beginning with a $25 gift in 1983, a generous individual made a total of 279 monthly gifts of $25 or $30 for a total of 279 monthly gifts over a 22 year period. The donor passed away and one year later [the] organization received a $25,000 bequest. Total value of these 280 gifts: $31,250!"

Whatever you call them—monthly givers, committed givers, sustainers, direct debits, Friends of, Circles of, Champions, Partners—the point is to get started. Now.

PART 5

Do the Math

20

What's Your Retention Rate and Why It Matters

Even if you're not into numbers, the inescapable truth is that your organization depends on donors. As a result, your retention rate is the fundamental indicator of how well you're performing in the eyes of your constituents.

In most cases, high retention is an indicia of high satisfaction, loyalty, and commitment; low retention, the opposite.

Donors (but also volunteers, advocates, activists, or any group of constituents) ultimately vote with their feet (and checkbooks). Displeased, unimpressed, or disappointed with you, they simply stop giving or volunteering and drop out—a sure sign any organization is failing in basic relationship management. And, with a million-plus nonprofits in the United States, donors have plenty of other choices.

For at least the past ten years—starting long before the Great Recession of 2008 and continuing through today—donor acquisition has grown increasingly expensive.

During this same period, first-year retention rates have declined to the point where, on average, nearly three out of four newly acquired donors leave by the end of the first year.

The result of this hemorrhaging boils down to this: for many organizations—and no part of the sector has escaped the decline—the financial return on acquiring new donors is now so poor it's no longer feasible to replace the flood of defectors.

The retention bucket is not only leaky, donors are pouring out of it in torrents.

Unfortunately, many CEOs and boards are either unaware of the importance of retention or they persist in measuring success by the somewhat meaningless metric of how many *new* donors are brought in each year.

Of course it's essential to continue acquiring new donors. But too great a focus on acquisition can be a warning sign of eventual failure. That's because it can blind you to the importance of the process that *must occur immediately following acquisition*. Namely, focusing on donor commitment, increasing donor value, and ensuring a high retention rate.

In turn, this obsession with acquiring donors usually means, somewhat ironically, that new supporters won't be treated as the long-term asset they represent and thus will be lost to attrition. Money wasted, the organization's future compromised.

What's Your Retention Rate?

Just as most of us are aware of our vital signs, such as blood pressure, cholesterol, and heart rate, every nonprofit executive should know his or her organization's *donor retention rate*.

It's easy to calculate.

Step 1: Count the total number of donors who gave in your most recent calendar or fiscal year.

Step 2: Divide the number of donors who made a donation in year 2 by the total in Step 1.

Step 3: Multiply the result from Step 2 by 100 to obtain your retention rate as a percentage.

For example, if 100 donors gave last year, and only 50 of the same donors made a gift this year, your overall retention rate would be 50 percent.

In addition to calculating the number or percentage of donors retained, you can also calculate your *revenue retention rate*. This metric is particularly helpful in spotting retention problems in the critical first two years of a donor's life with your organization.

For example, if 100 new donors gave you $50 each, you received $5,000 from the acquisition campaign. If in the following year 25 of those 100 donors upgraded a bit and each gave an additional $60, you received another $1,500. Your *donor retention rate* was 25 percent (25 divided by 100) and your *revenue retention rate* was 30 percent ($1,500 divided by $5,000).

Although there are several reasons to be concerned about a low retention rate, the most obvious is financial. Viewed simply in dollar terms, organizations with low rates of retention are throwing away thousands or even millions of dollars.

As Adrian Sargeant points out in his classic *Building Donor Loyalty*, "Even a 10% increase in donor retention can increase the lifetime value of the donor database by 200%."

Let me expand on that point. Currently the average retention rate in the United States is 41 percent calculated as an average multi-year percentage. That means that each year 59 out of every 100 donors leave and 41 stay.

Using an illustration prepared by Adrian Sargeant and the researchers at Bloomerang.co, let's see what happens to donation totals if the retention rate is increased by 10 percentage points. The illustration uses the example of 5,000 donors who give an average annual gift of $200.

TOTAL RETURN FOR A
10% DIFFERENCE IN RETENTION

Cumulative effect over 14 years

Year	Original Retention Rate: 41%				Improved Retention Rate: 51%		
	Donors	**Avg Gift**	**Total**		**Donors**	**Avg Gift**	**Total**
1	5,000	$200.00			5,000	$200.00	
2	2,050	$220.00	$451,000		2,550	$220.00	$561,000
3	841	$242.00	$203,000		1,301	$242.00	$314,721
4	345	$266.20	$91,734		663	$266.20	$176,558
5	141	$292.82	$41,372		338	$292.82	$99,049
6	58	$322.10	$18,659		173	$322.10	$55,567
7	24	$354.31	$8,415		88	$354.31	$31,173
8	10	$389.74	$3,795		45	$389.74	$17,488
9	4	$428.72	$1,712		23	$428.72	$9,811
10	2	$471.59	$772		12	$471.59	$5,504
11	-	-	-		6	$518.75	$3,088
12	-	-	-		3	$570.62	$1,732
13	-	-	-		2	$627.69	$972
14	-	-	-		1	$690.45	$545

Original Rate Total: $820.859   **Improved Rate Total: $1,277,208**

Total Increased Funds: $456,349

Source: Bloomerang.co

As the table above illustrates, the organization with a retention rate of 51 percent will raise literally hundreds of thousands more than the nonprofit with a retention rate of 41 percent.

In addition, the 10 percent improvement—attributable to some combination of better donor service, better messaging, and a proper thank you process—yields an increase in the number of years the original donors stay with the organization: four full years longer.

The Sargeant/Bloomerang analysis, confirmed by studies conducted by DonorVoice in the United States and the United Kingdom, reveal that organizations that take steps to retain and move their donors to a level of high commitment can improve their bottom lines by as much as $250,000 for every 1,000 donors over a three-year period.

And even if you assume that 10 percent or even 20 percent of the additional funds raised were invested in making the improvements that caused more donors to stay with you—let's assume $90,000—you come out way ahead both in terms of net income and increased retention and commitment for years to come

Few fundraising investments produce a greater return than those made for the purpose of increasing retention rates. Prove it for yourself by doing a quick calculation for your organization.

21

Lifetime Value: The Ultimate Metric

We've all heard the parable of the policeman who spots a drunk searching under a streetlight. He asks the inebriated fellow what he's lost.

The drunk says he's misplaced his keys and they both look under the streetlight together. After a few minutes the policeman asks the man if he's sure he lost the keys here. The drunk replies, "No, I lost them in the park."

"Then why are we searching here?" asks the stymied cop.

"Because the light's better," the drunk replies.

It's human nature. We all look for things where the light is better, rather than where we're most likely to find them.

That's why so many of us and our boards, CEOs, and CFOs persist in using such metrics as the "cost of fundraising" or "overhead," which have little value when it comes to making longer-term fundraising and investment decisions.

An all-too-familiar scenario at nonprofit board meetings is when the new donor acquisition report is given and the board learns that $60 was spent to acquire a $30 donor.

To the uninitiated, the cost of fundraising for that acquisition campaign appears to be 200 percent more than the amount of the contributions received, or a negative two to one return on investment (ROI).

The board bristles, the CEO can't explain it adequately, and future acquisition efforts are curtailed. The organization goes into a death spiral that comes from not replacing enough lapsed or lost donors through ongoing acquisition efforts.

The end result, as Australian fundraiser Sean Triner puts it, "is that in the end this obsession with cost of fundraising and Return on Investment (ROI) damages our ability to make the world a better place."

This narrow focus on short-term costs and income occludes an organization's vision of the big, long-term picture. By using wrong measurements, we lose sight of the forest and focus instead on the trees.

But rather than stagger around in the forest, confused by short-term metrics, let's focus on lifetime value (LTV) and why it's such an essential tool in the fundraiser's measuring kit.

What Is Lifetime Value?

Over the long haul, lifetime value is the most significant measure for benchmarking and steering your fundraising efforts.

In fact, as Charlie Hulme, head of DonorVoice's U.K. operation puts it, "Unless you believe you'll find the cure/right the wrong/ feed every child with your next appeal it's unethical not to focus on lifetime value."

Yet it remains one of the most overlooked and least understood metrics in our trade—even though it's one of the easiest to figure out.

Once you know a donor's lifetime value, you'll better understand how to allocate your resources, both in terms of donor acquisition and donor retention.

A Simple Way to Estimate Lifetime Value

An easy-to-understand, commercial example of the lifetime value concept is that of a gym member who spends $20 every month for three years. The three-year lifetime value of that customer would be $720 ($20 × 12 months × 3 years = $720 in total revenue).

You can see even from this example why many health clubs offer a free starter membership. Gym owners know that as long as they spend less than $240 to acquire a new member (the amount the member will pay in the first year—$20 a month × 12 months), the customer will prove profitable in a relatively short amount of time.

This is the same way our boards, CFOs, and fundraisers should view the investment in acquiring new donors.

I've attended countless board meetings where the development director attempts to explain why the organization is spending $30 to acquire a new donor who contributes only $15 with her first gift. "That's an unacceptable 200 percent cost of fundraising!" the treasurer angrily exclaims.

But what if every one of those new donors has a five-year lifetime value of $300?

Instead of losing $15 per donor, the acquisition effort actually produces a valuable asset worth $270 per donor in gross income over the next five years.

That's a 20 percent per year return on investment. Probably a lot better annual return than the organization is getting from its endowment portfolio.

Happy board. Happy CEO. You're a rock star!

This leads to the important question: do you know the three-, five-, ten-, or even twenty-year lifetime value of your donors or members?

Fortunately, it's easy to calculate when you put the actual or estimated numbers into the following equation:

Average $ amount of a donor's gift to your organization

Multiplied by the number of repeat gifts per year by that donor

Multiplied by the average number of years your donors remain on your active file

The result equals gross lifetime value.

(You can arrive at the net lifetime value by deducting the costs of soliciting and servicing the donor over the period of time you're measuring.)

Note: If you don't want to use your own pencil and paper to calculate LTV, you can go online and use Harvard University's free calculator (http://hbsp.harvard.edu/multimedia/flashtools/cltv/index.html).

It's not important how you do it, just that you do it!

22

How Do Lifetime Value and Retention Connect?

The longer you retain donors, the likelier they are to increase their commitment to you. Increased longevity gives you more time to prove your reliability and consistency, more time to thank, more opportunities to recognize and involve the donor, and more time to upgrade the size and types of his or her gift, perhaps eventually securing a bequest.

My friend Fraser Green, a Canadian fundraiser whom I suspect believes donor loyalty and retention are more important than ice hockey or maple syrup, poses an interesting question in his book *3D Philanthropy* (Civil Sector Press, 2011):

"How much would you bid for a busload of donors?"

The answer illustrates the combined power of retention and lifetime value.

I have a busload of 50 donors outside in the parking lot. Each one of these donors is going to make 1.3 gifts of $45 per year for the next 7 years. I'm now going to auction these donors off—what am I bid?

Let me make it even easier. Each donor is going to give a total of $409.50 in his "lifetime" with your organization. The busload is worth $20,475.

Fraser then shares some additional information about three of the donors—identical triplets who all give to the same hypothetical charity.

Janice makes her gifts through the mail. She stays active with your charity for four years before she lapses. Her average annual gift is $40. Janice's (gross) lifetime value is $160. This is pretty typical.

Joanne starts out the same as Janice and gives the same amount through the mail—except that after four years she converts to monthly giving. She stays on as a $14 per month donor for another eight years before she eventually lapses. Joanne's lifetime value is $1,504—ten times the value of her sister!

Jacqueline starts out the same as her sisters with four years of direct mail giving. She then follows Joanne with eight years of monthly giving. But, Jacqueline does something more. She decides to leave 5% of her estate to the charity in her will which amounts to $20,000. Jacqueline's total lifetime value to your charity is $21,504.

Jacqueline's value is 14 times greater than Joanne's—and 134 times greater than Janice's!

You see, the formula for fundraising magic is simple: retention + commitment = increased lifetime value.

Let's take a coffee break.

What if I told you Starbucks spends $18.40 to get a new customer to spend $4.25 for a Caramel Frappacino®?

Unless you understand the power of retention coupled with lifetime value, you'd likely say Starbucks is foolish. That is, until you learned that the twenty-year lifetime value of a Starbucks customer is $14,090!

That's why, for the same reason, Amazon spends $240 to acquire a customer for its $69 Kindle, why insurance companies pay more than 100 percent of the first year's premium to acquire a policy holder, and on and on.

And that's also why in addition to making the initial acquisition investment, these successful companies spend additional money in customer service aimed at increasing satisfaction and loyalty.

Unfortunately, many boards and CEOs don't understand how cost of acquisition and lifetime value combine to provide the true value and return on the acquisition investment. Take a look at the illustration below reflecting the acquisition investment/return for Starbucks and ask yourself if the name wasn't on the chart would your board or CEO approve?

INVESTING IN DONOR VS. CUSTOMER ACQUISITION

What Would Your Board Say?

- Organization "A" spends $24.30 for a first time gift of $5.90 for a loss of $18.40

- Organization "B" spends $250 for a first time gift of $110 for a loss of $140

- Organization "C" spends $320 for a first time gift of $199 for a loss of $121

The Power of Lifetime Value

Investment:
$**18**⁴⁰

Return:
$**14,090**
Over 20 Years

The same principles of investment in acquisition, donor service, and retention hold true for virtually all nonprofit organizations.

Failure to invest substantially in the acquisition and care of new donors is a certain prescription for extinction.

A well-run donor care or retention program is the wellspring, the feeder track, the seed corn (call it what you will) of a long-term financial development process that, if properly measured and executed, leads to highly profitable monthly giving, mid-level giving, upgrading to major gifts, and eventually sizable bequests or other planned gifts.

Each of these programs adds to the lifetime value of a donor base.

Only by calculating the fundamental metrics of retention and lifetime value for your organization will you have what you need to design and steer an effective and growing fundraising program.

PART 6

Donor Retention Made Easy and Final Thoughts

23

Cliff Notes for Retention

The other day when I dropped off my pickup for a tune-up I noticed a sign above the workbench of my favorite mechanic: "I can explain it to you, but I can't make you understand it."

That's when it occurred to me that perhaps there are many well-intentioned people who don't really have the time or temperament to tackle and understand the entire process of donor retention outlined in this book.

So, unlike the process suggestions in chapter 19, "Easy Retention Wins for Everyone," this chapter is basically the cliff notes version for the whole book. It aims to provide a basic *do this* list while skipping over any detailed explanation of *why*.

This is a list of quick, easy, and inexpensive steps that can be implemented immediately to improve retention. It's not all inclusive. It represents an effort to spotlight those actions likely to matter most and produce the quickest improvement.

- **Measure the vital signs**

There's no point in doing anything about retention if you can't measure the overall effects of your actions. So, before all else, take a few minutes to calculate your organization's first-year and multi-year retention rates and the lifetime value of your donors.

These are easy calculations to make, and chapters 20 and 21 show you how. A year from now, after you've applied some of the first aid techniques in this chapter, go back and see how much your retention rate has improved.

- **Focus first on basics, especially your**
organization's mindset regarding donors

In essence, if you want to improve retention, all you need are good manners, an understanding of human nature, and a true sense of appreciation for the donor.

Here's an inspiring summary of how one small organization puts relationship basics to work as reported by Stephen Best of the group Animal Alliance Environment Voters (AAEV). Perhaps your organization is too large to take all these personal steps, or perhaps some don't fit your style. But what is universally important for every organization regardless of size is the attitude toward donors reflected here.

> We retain over 90% of people who have given more than one gift. We lose people usually because of personal issues: financial problems, health problems, family discord, and

death. Rarely is it due to issues with the organization or its campaigns.

For new supporters we retain about 70%. However, because our organization is small we've done no acquisition fundraising since 1999. . . . all new AAEV supporters have joined due to word of mouth and earned media. Despite no direct response fundraising, the organization has grown, but more importantly net income has increased dramatically.

What's the secret? Genuinely appreciating that supporters are those rare people who actually make our world a better place. We work for them, and everything we do reflects that understanding. Our supporters and our volunteers are our family, all 5,000 of them and we treat them like a community of friends, because that's what, in fact, they are. This attitude is shared by everyone in the organization.

People who don't appreciate how special donors are don't last long at AAEV. Every donation is thanked, hand-written by a volunteer on the day we receive the gift.

Our executive director spends time on the phone with any supporter who wants to speak to her. Any supporter's complaint or concern is handled personally by phone, usually by the executive director. The fact is complaints are, generally, the best retention opportunity an organization ever gets.

Stephen goes on to offer some insights and admonitions for every nonprofit.

I've yet to encounter any organization small or large prepared to treat supporters with the respect and admiration they deserve. Generally (there are a few notable exceptions) fundraisers, directors, managers, and even activists and program managers want a quick, cheap 'business' or 'technological' or 'creative' fix that produces a magical result in the same budget cycle—the future be damned.

More troubling is that a fix is usually wanted that can be done via the Internet so that no real contact is required. Most of the nonprofit community usually treat supporters, particularly small contributors, as a necessary evil not as people who'd like nothing better than to invite you to dinner.

Stephen's Golden Rule for retention: "To succeed, treat every supporter as you would have him or her treat you."

- **Say "thank you" quickly and personally**

If you want a higher retention rate, saying thank you is a prime starting point for signaling to the donor, "You matter to our organization. Your gift counts and makes a difference."

In chapter 16 we saw that promptly and personally thanking donors is one of the top seven key drivers of commitment. It's also one of the easiest holes to fix in your leaky retention bucket.

To begin with, you'll be miles ahead of your competition if you even bother to thank your donors. Over the years, survey after donor survey has shown that as many as 60 percent of nonprofits don't even bother to acknowledge or thank their donors.

Is it any wonder that at least 13 percent of donors who defect attribute their reason for leaving to the fact that they never were thanked?

Volumes have been written about the importance of effective and timely thank-yous. A great resource with plenty of examples is Lisa Sargent's Thank You Letter Clinic appearing on the Showcase of Fundraising Innovation and Inspiration (http://www.sofii.org/article/how-to-write-a-better-thank-you-letter-and-why-it-matters).

Here are the questions Lisa suggests you ask about your gift acknowledgment and thank-you process:

- How soon after a gift is received do we send a thank-you letter?
- Do we note the amount of the donation?
- For gift memberships, do we send notices to both the giver and the receiver?
- Do we recognize long-term and repeat donors? If not, is our system capable of this?
- What kind of donor feedback have we received on thank yous?

It's not enough that thank-yous in one form or another are sent in a timely fashion. The quality of those messages matter. They must convey genuine appreciation and also show the impact of the gift, assuring donors that their gifts are making a difference. In short, a generic computer-generated thank-you letter, even if mailed the day the gift is received, is inadequate.

- **Pick up the phone**

A decade ago Penelope Burk in her book *Donor-Centered Fundraising* (2003, Burk & Associates Ltd) noted that personally telephoning new donors improved first-year revenue retention by some 40 percent. Years later Chuck Longfield, founder of Target Analytics and Blackbaud's chief scientist, conducted a large test to confirm this.

Here's what Chuck found:

- Simply calling and thanking new donors resulted in approximately 40 percent more revenue in the following year.
- Even leaving a thank-you message increased giving, but less than the 40 percent increase from those who were directly reached. (Chuck has since done more testing and determined that it's worth calling back at least once more before leaving a voice mail.)

A proper thank-you sets the stage for what many consider to be the critical factor in predicting longer-term retention—the second gift.

The sooner you thank a new donor the sooner you can ask for the next gift. Don't let what I call the "artificial barrier of good taste and dignity" stand in your way. That is, resist the notion drilled into us since childhood that somehow it's impolite to ask again so soon.

If you're looking for a canary in the coal mine test on how you're doing on retention, the percentage of second gifts you receive from new or first-time donors is probably the quickest, most reliable sign. If you can significantly increase the number of second gifts you'll also see a significant increase in retention rates and growth in the lifetime value of your donors.

- **Put more money into retention—today**

It has always struck me as strange that we budget tens of thousands of dollars—even millions—on acquisition while completely ignoring any allocation of funds for retention.

Take for example a proper investment in what we just discussed— the thank-you process. The fact that so many organizations view their acknowledgment/thank-you/welcome efforts as a cost rather than an essential part of the process of acquiring and retaining a new donor makes absolutely no sense.

A donor whose first contribution is ignored or improperly acknowledged is likely headed for the exit. The chances of him or her making a second gift are vastly diminished. From the very start, we have failed in the essential first step of relationship building—establishing a feeling of reliability on the donor's part. And as we've seen, without the twin pillars of reliability and consistency, the essential ingredient for retention—trust—is missing.

The same is true for other essential functions. Activities such as donor service—the proper and careful recording of names and addresses, the prompt attention to inquiries and complaints, a skilled and friendly representative at the other end of the service center's phone line.

If an organization is willing to invest $50 to acquire a $25 dollar donor, why wouldn't it budget at least an additional $5 or $6 to make certain that new donor is properly thanked and welcomed with her or his name spelled properly? Why not spend the money to phone and thank these first-year donors, thus assuring 40 percent more income from them next year?

Investing in retention is so important that as a matter of practice I recommend that the cost for properly placing new donors on the right road to solid retention be built into the acquisition costs at the outset.

- **Start discriminating**

All donors are not equal. At least not when it comes to building retention and lifetime value.

The sooner you identify your best donors and where they come from, the sooner you'll be on the road to higher retention and increased lifetime value. That's because you'll be able to invest more time and money in the donors who have demonstrated their loyalty and commitment and less in those who haven't.

1. Identifying and engaging the best current donors

There are a variety of ways to measure who among your donors are the most committed and the most deserving of additional time and effort. The most accurate and predictive way is to score them using the donor commitment scoring system outlined in chapter 12.

In lieu of an empirical scoring approach, however, there are some signs of commitment and loyalty you should look for:

- Length of time as an active donor with your organization;
- Size of gifts, including whether the gifts have been trending upward; and

- Involvement or engagement. Donors who both give and volunteer are generally more committed than those who just volunteer.

2. *Spotting signs they care*

While not proof positive of high commitment or loyalty, there are some additional signals that may be helpful in identifying your better donors.

- If a donor has taken the time to complain
- If a donor has reached out to change his/her address
- If a donor has gone to the effort of having his or her gift matched by his or her employer
- If the donor has attended a conference call briefing or actual meeting

A word of caution on these signs, however. Be aware of what statisticians call the confounding variable. In the example of the donor who calls you with a change of address, there could be a third variable that confounds the relationship. Perhaps she took the time to call because you thanked her in a timely manner, or told a moving story about someone you helped, or otherwise reinforced the notion that your organization is on top of its mission. The question at the forefront of your mind should always be "What did we do that created the donor's positive attitude?"

3.   Additional proof they care

I also recommend you take the time to calculate the lifetime value of this special, more caring group of donors. When you do, you'll quickly see why it's worth spending more time and money on them.

- **Signs donors may soon leave you**

Just as you'll see indications of a donor's high level of commitment, there are telltale signs that a donor is preparing to abandon ship.
   Some signals to watch for:

- Downgrading of giving levels
- Unsubscribing from your various e-mail and e-newsletter lists
- Stopping a recurring gift like a monthly sustainer
- Negative comments in social media
- Canceling an event reservation

You should be able to use your organization's database, CRM, or other software to filter your donors to spot many of these signs. Some software developers, alert to the issue of retention, have built in or preprogrammed reports for this purpose. For example, Bloomerang (https://bloomerang.co/image/uploads/ProductOverview.pdf) has engaged loyalty expert Adrian Sargent and built into its software an engagement meter that alerts organizations to slips or improvements in their donors' engagement levels.
   Once you know who's most likely to defect, you can decide what steps to take to hold onto these donors or whether the time and

money are perhaps better spent on bonding the most committed donors even closer.

• **Putting new water into your less leaky bucket**

Once you've stopped the bleeding or, more accurately, plugged the biggest holes in your retention bucket, you can turn your attention to other significant actions to improve retention.

1. Check the source of new donors

The quality of new donors you bring in is important. Look at the original source of donors who have proven to be the most valuable both in terms of length of retention and lifetime value.

For example, if you acquire donors mainly by direct mail, you'll find some lists produce higher-quality donors than others. You won't be able to tell this from the initial response rate. You have to determine how well these donors performed once you acquired them.

Pay similar attention to donors acquired through events, online, in print ads, and other channels. Avoid using the poor performing (from a retention and value standpoint) sources of new donors in the future.

2. Cooperative data banks and exchanging lists

Many direct mail-oriented organizations exchange their donor lists or place their names in cooperative data banks used for acquisition campaigns. While this practice in and of itself can be beneficial from an acquisition standpoint, it also has substantial drawbacks that can negatively affect retention.

For example, when you make your donors available to other organizations, you're opening yourself up to competition and the consequent loss of those donors to other groups using your mailing list. And the more frequently your list is used, the greater the opportunity for loss.

Take a look at the frequency with which you are exchanging names or allowing them to be used by a cooperative data base and determine whether there's any significant loss each time those names are used by others.

- **Focus on metrics that matter**

By my definition, an important metric is one that triggers the question "What should I do differently to improve?"

Here are my picks for metrics that really matter:

1. *Acquisition metrics*

At the risk of boring the non-arithmetic (but pleasing the CFO), I believe there's a far better way to assemble a more meaningful acquisition response report—one that actually helps you steer into the future and pay more attention to retention:

From the number of new donors you acquired, subtract the percentage you historically lose by year 2. For example, say you brought in 1,000 donors from a 100,000-piece mailing (a 1 percent response rate). Now, drop 70 percent of them because history shows that's how many won't give in year 2.

Next, take the total money you spent on acquisition, let's say $75,000, and deduct the money you raised, let's say $20,000, with an average gift of $20.

Finally, divide the number of acquired donors (1,000) by the number of donors who will remain in year 2 (300).

The equation looks like this:

$75,000 (spent) – $20,000 (raised) = $55,000 ÷ 300 stay-around donors = $183.33.

To break even on this acquisition mailing, you'll need to raise $183.33 from each of the 300 donors you acquired.

The questions triggered from this more realistic metric are "What fundraising plan for a single donor will raise $183 over the next two or three years?" "Does the plan make sense?" and "Can the plan be scaled in volume?"

I suggest two or three or even more years for your plan. It's unrealistic to expect you can both acquire and securely bond a new donor in the first year. Unless you're prepared to nurture new donors over a multi-year period, you probably shouldn't be investing in their acquisition in the first place.

In my experience with literally hundreds of nonprofits, those in charge of acquisition almost never deal adequately with this key metric.

2.   Key retention metrics

There are only a few measurements that matter when it comes to retention and ensuring that your efforts on track.

- *Number of new donors making a second gift.* This is a har-binger, if not a dead-on predictor of the retention rate and lifetime value (LTV) you're likely to experience.
- *Number of new donors retained into the second year.* Fixing the leaky bucket of retention begins with new donors—what we do to hold them, what we do to lose them. Survey or talk to your best donors to find out what you're doing that pleases them. Likewise, ask those who defected why they did so.
- *Multiple-year retention rates.* Same as above, but by tracking these figures year-by-year, you can spot additional trends, problems, and opportunities for improving your program.
- *Lifetime value of a donor (LTV).* At the end of the day, all the actions you take to improve retention, average gift, and donor commitment will be reflected in the LTV of each donor and all donors collectively. This is the key metric on which to benchmark, guide, and track the success or fail-ure of your intermediate and long-term strategies.

- **Clean up your files**

If, on his weekend off, a fundraiser lost a $100 bill while hiking, he'd probably devote the rest of the day to searching for it. Unfor-tunately, too often that motivation doesn't extend to the office. As basic and obvious as the maintenance of correct donor information is, countless organizations ignore its importance.

There are a multitude of low-cost services that will help you keep your records up to date. I've listed some on this book's website at www.retentionfundraising.com.

- **Ignore the trivial. Remember the donor.**

Concentrating on the basics of donor care is hard work. As such, it's easy to avoid—and, besides, it's a lot more fun to divert our attention to the new and shiny.

Instead of continually searching for some magic bullet, particularly one that comes as an app on a smart phone, we constantly need to remind ourselves that we're here in service to the donor—the driving engine of good works.

As you work to apply retention first aid to your program, there's no better guide than keeping the vision of what Damian O'Broin, an Irish fundraiser, calls a "Dream Donor" in mind:

> Please find enclosed a checque . . . to pay for raffle tickets. . . . Oxfam is my primary charity. Castelebar, the place where I work, has an Oxfam shop and I can go in and make an extra donation for a specific purpose either because disaster has struck somewhere or for a special occasion in my own life . . . .
>
> I would like to let you know that I give money to Oxfam in good faith. There are many people who live in dire circumstances and I trust Oxfam and its employees/volunteers to do the best for them that they are able and to do so within the given circumstances. I like it that Oxfam is a large organization so that they have expertise in various fields and a large body of personnel to draw upon. You are unable as an individual to deliver aid to whoever needs it. That would be impossible and very wasteful.
>
> The money you received from me is real money—with that I mean, if I didn't give the money to you, I wouldn't

have difficulty finding another use for it. What I am really trying to say is this: I trust you to spend money wisely and carefully and give aid appropriately with consideration to people's background. I don't expect Oxfam employees to work for nothing. They need to be properly paid.

I am proud to support Oxfam and I know that puts a responsibility on all Oxfam personnel.

Amen to Damian.

24

Final Thoughts

I s retention really the problem our organizations are most interested in fixing?

I'd argue that the answer is categorically "No!"

This poses a dilemma, since I've devoted this entire book to the proposition that it *is* the biggest problem, and the key solution.

Deep down I suspect most experienced fundraisers—particularly direct response fundraisers—believe that acquisition is a lot easier than retention. They simply don't buy the adage that it's easier to keep a donor than to find a new one.

And, in truth, donor acquisition *is* still easier than retention. Not less expensive, not more valuable, but easier. Retention requires time to analyze and measure. Time to improve donor experiences. Time to test and evaluate improvements. A lot more time compared to the very short-term tactics and measurements involved in acquisition.

Surveying your donors' attitudes, creating effective messages, providing good donor service—these combined activities require considerable effort and planning. Few organizations have either the stomach or the resolve.

I opened this book with a plea for change, and I must close in the same way. We cannot expect a brighter future by repeating the same tactics, recycling the same thinking again and again.

What will lead us to a brighter and more productive future with our donors are different inputs, grounded not just in emotion and hunch but in theory and math. My hope is that this book guides us in that direction and that different outputs will ensue as a result.

I wish you patience, persistence, and success.

Appendices

APPENDIX A

Suggested (Short) Reading and Resource List

Plenty of books, courses, and websites have been published on the specific tools and tactics essential for fundraising success. My goal here is to recommend a short reading list focused mainly on philosophies, strategies, and tactics that go to the heart of donor retention and lifetime value and what it takes to create a donor-centered organization.

- Ken Burnett, *Relationship Fundraising: A Donor-Based Approach to the Business of Raising Money*, 2nd ed. (John Wiley & Sons, 2002). This is the classic when it comes to understanding what's involved in building solid relationships with donors through effective communication. Packed with case examples, donor profiles, and more than 200 action points. A must read.
- Adrian Sargeant and Elaine Jay, *Building Donor Loyalty: The Fundraiser's Guide to Increasing Lifetime Value* (San Francisco: Jossey-Bass, 2004). Another classic that bridges solid academic

research with practical, illustrative case studies. Drawing on data from research on more than 20,000 donors, the authors demonstrate the power of effective donor-retention strategies and set forth the factors that can build donor loyalty.

- Harvey McKinnon, *Hidden Gold: How Monthly Giving Will Build Donor Loyalty, Boost Your Organization's Income, and Increase Financial Stability* (Chicago: Bonus Books, 1999). Building a successful monthly giving program puts you miles ahead in terms of both donor retention and lifetime value. If you are recruiting monthly donors, this book will help you build a solid program. Harvey McKinnon is acknowledged around the world as an expert in monthly giving. Hidden Gold is the guide.

- Jeff Brooks, *The Fundraiser's Guide to Irresistible Communications: Real-World, Field-Tested Strategies for Raising More Money* (Medfield, MA: Emerson & Church, 2012). Not only is Jeff's guide jam-packed with practical advice but it's written by a leading advocate of donor-focused fundraising. In a world where too many pay lip service to becoming "donor-centric," Jeff gives us the "why" and "how" of creating copy that puts the donor first and foremost.

- Tom Ahern, *Making Money from Donor Newsletters: The How-To Guide to Extraordinary Results* (Medfield, MA: Emerson & Church, 2013). Rediscover the "how," "what," and "why" of a 3,000-year-old technology—words and pictures on paper—and how when properly employed they can unlock a treasure trove of contributions and donor loyalty. A properly prepared donor newsletter will add heaps to your bottom line, bring a tsunami of joy to your donors, and boost the lifetime value and retention rates of your organization's donors to new heights.

- Tom Ahern and Simone Joyaux, *Keep Your Donors: The Guide to Better Communications & Stronger Relationships* (Hoboken, NJ: John Wiley & Sons, 2008). Two masters in the field of nonprofit organizational development, donor relationships, and communications have created what amounts to a wonderful reference and fun-to-read guide to best practices. Best of all, it's a powerful antidote to the narrow focus on technique and technology at the expense of relationship building.

- *The Donor Retention Project* (TheRetentionProject.com, 2013). Not a book but rather a fascinating collection of online or printed guides, along with CDs containing interviews with retention practitioners. Based on current donor-retention research, the series contains strategies and templates aimed at improving retention rates.

- Lisa Sargent, *The Thank-You Letter Clinic* (SOFII.org, 2014). As you've seen in the chapter "Retention Wins for Everyone," the thank-you process is a big factor in better retention. Visit Lisa Sargent's *Thank-You Letter Clinic* to find a treasure trove of how-to advice and thank-you letters you can swipe.

- RetentionFundraising.com, the website for this book, contains additional reading, other resources, and updates on the latest research on donor commitment and retention.

APPENDIX B

More Detail on Marketing Relationship Theory

There is a sizable body of work by academics and practitioners who've devised a framework called *relationship theory* to determine and describe the dynamics and essential ingredients of both personal and commercial relationships.

Today, commercial marketers have spent literally billions of dollars applying relationship theory. The research behind the conclusions and recommendations in *Retention Fundraising* are rooted in it.

For a deeper understanding of relationship theory, I recommend reading the following. I've included only a short representative sampling to show the evolution from the theory itself . . . to the application of the theory in the world of commerce . . . and finally to the nonprofit donor sector.

First came the seminal piece of research:

Robert Morgan and Shelby Hunt, "The Commitment-Trust Theory of Relationship Marketing." In 1994 this paper in the *Journal of Marketing* rocked the marketing world by putting forth a major shift in marketing theory. The authors hypothesized and proved that successful relationship marketing requires both commitment and trust.

You can download the study at http://www.jstor.org/discover/10.2 307/1252308?uid=3739256&uid=2129&uid=2134&uid=2481820877.

Three years later, Susan Fournier of the Harvard Business School demonstrated how the Morgan and Hunt research applies in the consumer world in "Consumers and Their Brands: Developing Relationship Theory in Consumer Research." Published in the *Journal of Consumer Research*, Fournier's article is a good introduction to how relationship theory is being tested and used in the commercial world. In the years since "Consumers and Their Brands" appeared, consumer product companies have increasingly embraced relationship theory in their marketing and customer-loyalty programs.

You can download the article at http://bear.warrington.ufl.edu/weitz/mar7786/articles/fournier%20(1998).pdf.

Nearly twenty years later, market researcher Kevin Schulman summarized how all of this applies to the nonprofit sector in "Applying Relationship Theory to Donor Stewardship." Prepared for DonorVoice, this paper outlines how relationship-theory practices from the for-profit world work equally for nonprofits and provides step-by-step methods for improving retention and commitment, along with the reasoning behind those practices.

You can download this white paper at http://www.slideshare.net/kschulman14/donor-relationship-management.

APPENDIX C

**Using Lifetime Value as Your Fundraising
GPS to Boost Your Bottom Line**

Chapters 21 and 22 focus on lifetime value (LTV) and why it's an essential tool in the fundraiser's measuring kit.

A quick recap: Lifetime value is the most significant measure for benchmarking and steering your fundraising efforts over the long haul. It's also one of the most overlooked and least understood metrics in our trade—even though it's one of the easiest to figure out.

Why is the lifetime value number so important? Mainly because it'll give you an idea of how much income you can expect from a particular donor or group of donors. Knowing this figure will help you decide how much to spend to acquire those donors for your organization in the first place.

Once you know how frequently a donor gives and how much he or she contributes, you'll better understand how to allocate your resources in terms of both donor acquisition and donor retention efforts—the ongoing investments and actions needed to increase donors' value by building their loyalty and commitment. And, over time, by watching the lifetime value number rise or fall you'll know if you're on track.

The Simplest Way to Estimate Lifetime Value

There are a variety of ways, some simple, some more complex, to calculate lifetime value. For now let's keep it simple. Put the actual or estimated (if you're in the planning stages or just starting out) numbers into the following equation:

(Average Value of a Contribution) × (Number of Repeat Contributions) × (Average Retention Time in Months or Years for a Typical Donor) = Gross Lifetime Value

(You can arrive at the Net Lifetime Value by deducting the costs of soliciting and servicing the donor over the period of time you're measuring.)

If you don't want to use your own pencil and paper to calculate LTV, you can go online and use Harvard University's free calculator at http://hbsp.harvard.edu/multimedia/flashtools/cltv/index.html.

Let's work through a few examples of how you can use LTV to develop effective strategies to improve the bottom line. Here is a table I'll be referring to in the examples, so you might want to place a paper clip on the page for easy reference.

EXAMPLE: ACQUISITION PROGRAM USING PREMIUMS

Premium-driven acquisition programs are notorious for their low average gifts and poor retention rates. But they're mighty attractive for boosting acquisition response rates—and that pleases boards and CEOs who don't know any better. (Note the 5 percent acquisition response rate in Year 1 in the table on page 168. Note also the low average gift and the low retention rate.)

Several possible strategies suggest themselves in a case like this. You could work on improving average gift size, the number of gifts per year, or retention rates. Because you understand the importance of retention, let's concentrate on that, plus let's add an online component with more personal e-mails, a more personal website, and some postal mail in the form of cultivation to boost retention.

Notice that nowhere in these figures is "Cost of Fundraising" or "ROI" indicated. That's because they're meaningless numbers. Of course our costs would go up, but so would our retention rates and our net income. So we draw up a plan and a set of assumptions based upon using a retention hypothesis.

Hypothesis: By increasing retention rates by 10 percent, Lifetime Value will dramatically improve. Our plan might look like this:

INVESTING IN RETENTION YIELDS BETTER RETURN

Planning to invest in retention yields a better return

	Acquisition Year	Year 2	Year 3
Donors	200,000	90,000	49,500
Retention Rate	45%	55%	54%
Acq. Resp Rate	5.0%		
Gifts Per Year	1.30	1.50	1.60
Average Gift	$11.00	$12.00	$13.00
Web Average	$16.00	$20.00	$24.00
Web Gifts Per Year	1.30	1.40	1.50
Web Givers	8%	12%	14%
Web Gifts	$332,800.00	$302,400.00	$249,480.00
Total Revenue	**$3,192,800.00**	**$1,922,400.00**	**$1,279,080.00**
Overhead	20%	20%	20%
Overhead Cost	$638,560.00	$384,480.00	$255,816.00
Email & Website	$150,000.00	$150,000.00	$150,000.00
Acquisition Mail	4,000,000		
Retention Mail		200,000	200,000
Appeal Mail	50,000	400,000	400,000
Cost Each	$0.42	$0.42	$0.42
Mail Costs	$1,701,000.00	$252,000.00	$252,000.00
Total Costs	**$2,489,560.00**	**$786,480.00**	**$657,816.00**
Net Profit	$703,240.00	$1,135,920.00	$621,264.00
Discount Rate	1.00	1.14	1.30
Net Present Value	$703,240.00	$986,421.00	$477,895.38
Cum. NPV	$703,240.00	$1,699,661.00	$2,177,556.44
Lifetime Value	**$3.52**	**$8.50**	**$10.89**

Comparing this retention plan with the original lifetime value calculations, we can see the difference. Clearly this strategy indicates a difference worth testing.

DIFFERENT LTV STRATEGIES WORTH TESTING

The difference may prove the plan is worth testing

	Acquisition Year	Year 2	Year 3
Old LTV	$0.30	$3.07	$4.17
New LTV	$3.52	$8.50	$10.89
Difference	$3.22	$5.43	$6.72
X 200,000	**$644,240.00**	**$1,085,573.00**	**$1,343,776.00**

How You Really Should Be Thinking About Acquisition

Whether you're spending $1 or $125 to acquire a new donor, chances are you aren't spending or investing enough. That's because almost no one calculates acquisition costs with lifetime value in mind.

Acquisition costs should be calculated not only by the front-end costs of postage, printing, mailing lists, and creative but also by the steps you need to take immediately after a prospect responds and throughout that critical first year. Let me explain.

Most respondents to an acquisition effort aren't yet donors; they're simply qualified leads who may eventually become donors. It's what you do to transform their status from lead to donor that's key to both lifetime value and your organization's future.

For example, if you're spending $800 per thousand pieces of mail and receiving a 1 percent response with a $20 average gift, that part of the acquisition process has so far cost $60 per new donor/lead:

1% of 1,000 = 10
10 × $20 = $200
$800 – $200 = $600 net contribution
$600 ÷ 10 donors/leads = $60 per donor/lead

What you do next determines whether and how fast this investment is recovered and then begins producing net income. If you do nothing but send out an acknowledgment and, say, four appeals per year, you might be able to recover an additional $20 per each lead during the first year. That still leaves you with at least a negative $40 per donor/lead for that year. Worse yet, given today's poor first-year retention rates, which average 25 percent or less, those original ten donors will dwindle to three or four the next year. And even though they'll retain at a higher rate in years two, three, and four, there's not much value dropping to the bottom line.

It's in this situation that phase two of a solid acquisition program must kick in. And by phase two, I mean the expenditure of additional funds in those first days/weeks after the lead's or donor's initial response.

How? Well, I'd certainly recommend spending at least an additional $5 or so on a thank-you phone call to welcome each new lead. This easy-to-execute and relative low-cost action will boost the first-year retention rate right then and there.

All of the testing I've done and all of the results I've seen from others indicate that retention rates go up an average of 20 to 24 percent thanks to that call. And often subsequent average gifts continue to increase as well.

Of course, if you're hounded by the ghost of fundraising costs, this bonding process may scare you, because it'll add another 15 or 20 percent to the cost of acquisition. But it's the best initial investment you can make in boosting lifetime value, because it boosts retention rates dramatically. You'll go into the second and subsequent years with far more donors giving higher average gifts.

If you don't have a plan—and the money set aside—for taking these critical first steps to converting a lead to a more loyal and permanent donor, you're really wasting money.

APPENDIX D

Go to the Movies. Change Your Organization's Mindset.

Designing and executing an effective donor-retention program almost always requires some change in an organization's mindset. Breaking down silos, focusing everyone's attention on donors, and budgeting for retention is tough work.

I have a suggestion for your next board meeting, retreat, staff conference, or wherever people are gathered to discuss your organization's future:

Eliminate 2 hours, 13 minutes of "done this, heard that" sessions from the agenda, serve free popcorn, and treat everyone to a screening of the movie *Moneyball*.

I'm serious.

Moneyball, the 2003 iconoclastic bestseller by Michael Lewis, was made into a popular and acclaimed movie starring Brad Pitt.

Moneyball, which is an effective study in counterproductive behaviors, deals not only with wins and losses but also with a man's quest to revolutionize a sport; someone who, in Lewis' words was willing "to rethink baseball: how it is managed . . . how it is played . . . and who is best suited to play it, and why."

That man was Billy Beane, the provocative general manager of the Oakland A's, who has unconventional ideas about what a team with limited resources can do to compete with such wealthy powerhouses as the New York Yankees.

Bean takes on the system by challenging the fundamental tenets of the game. He looks outside baseball's cherished dependence on the intuition of scouts and hires a brainy young number-crunching Harvard-educated economist to help him figure out a better way.

Armed with computer-driven statistical analysis long ignored by the baseball establishment, they go after players overlooked and dismissed by the business-as-usual baseball world for being too old, injured, or too much trouble, but all of whom have key skills that are universally undervalued.

And just as in every other specialized field of human endeavor, the detractors, the old-guard, and the high priests argue that this focus on numbers dehumanizes the game and ignores the intangibles that only trained scouts can see.

Although data analytics is an element in the story, that's not really what *Moneyball* is about. Instead, it's a real-life story of innovating, of changing your mindset to succeed. Or as Billy Beane puts it in the movie, "Adapt or die."

It took some time, but eventually most of professional baseball adopted the *Moneyball* mindset and strategy.

And so it is in today's world of nonprofit fundraising, communications, and management. More than ever survival depends on innovation, the willingness to challenge old assumptions, and, to no small degree, adopt a mindset that demands discovery and use of better metrics.

It's more than coincidence that *Moneyball* begins with a quote from Yankees star Mickey Mantle: "It's unbelievable how much you don't know about the game you've been playing all your life."

Ain't that the truth.

Copies of this and other books from the publisher are available at discount when purchased in quantity for boards of directors or staff. Call 508-359-0019 or visit www.emersonandchurch.com

Emerson
& Church
PUBLISHERS

15 Brook Street – Medfield, MA 02052
Tel. 508-359-0019 – Fax 508-359-2703
www.emersonandchurch.com